Death of a Holy Land

Death of a Holy Land

*Reflections in Contemporary
Israeli Fiction*

Rose L. Levinson

LEXINGTON BOOKS
Lanham • Boulder • New York • Toronto • Plymouth, UK

Published by Lexington Books
A wholly owned subsidiary of The Rowman & Littlefield Publishing Group, Inc.
4501 Forbes Boulevard, Suite 200, Lanham, Maryland 20706
www.rowman.com

10 Thornbury Road, Plymouth PL6 7PP, United Kingdom

British Library Cataloguing in Publication Information Available

Library of Congress Cataloging-in-Publication Data

Levinson, Rose L., 1941- author.
Death of a Holy Land : reflections in contemporary Israeli fiction / Rose L. Levinson.
pages cm
Includes bibliographical references and index.
ISBN 978-0-7391-7772-3 (cloth : alk. paper) -- ISBN 978-0-7391-7773-0 (electronic)
1. Israeli fiction--History and criticism. I. Title.
PJ5029.L48 2013
892.4'3709--dc23
2013010613

Printed in the United States of America

For David Berkow, z"l, beloved grandfather and teacher, and for David Jeffrey, beloved mate and teacher

Contents

Acknowledgments

Thanks to Roni Natov, first reader; Erin Hyman, invaluable editor; Nancy Herrick, precious healer; Victoria Costello, helpful consultant; David Jeffrey, unflagging everything. This is for the generations to come who gave light to the task, especially Tamsin, Alex, Joel and Freya Pasinios; Noam and Gadi Garfinkel; Amy and Matt Williams; Sara LeVee; Matt LeVee; Tadi Chirongoma.

PERMISSIONS

Excerpts from *Adam Resurrected* by Yoram Kaniuk. Copyright 1971 by Yoram Kaniuk. Used by permission of Grove/Atlantic, Inc. Any third party use of this material, outside of this publication, is prohibited.

Excerpts from *His Daughter* by Yoram Kaniuk. Copyright 1984 by Yoram Kaniuk. Reprinted by permission of George Braziller, Inc., New York. All rights reserved.

Excerpts from *Dolly City* by Orly Castel-Bloom. Trans. The Institute for the Translation of Hewbrew Literature. Copyright 1997. Reprinted by permission of Loki Books, Ltd.

Excerpts from *Human Parts* by Orly Castel-Bloom. Trans. Dalya Bilu. Copyright 2003 by Orly Castel-Bloom. Reprinted by permission of David R. Godine, Publisher.

Introduction

Loosening the Ties that Bind

This is an inquiry into contemporary Israeli culture. It explores contentious social issues through the works of four artists who live in a troubled country at a chaotic time. The fiction of these writers illuminates political, social, and communal circumstances that form the background for Israelis struggling to make sense of their interior lives and their relationships to others. Discussing these novels as a lens into Israel, the fictional works are viewed as cultural artifacts that provide insight into real-world concerns.

No sense of optimism prevails in the invented worlds of Yoram Kaniuk, Michal Govrin, Orly Castel-Bloom, and Zeruya Shalev. Taken together, their Israel is a far cry from the hopeful idealism of early settlers whose imaginations formed nascent visions of what a Jewish homeland would be. Neither does the Israel of these authors bear relation to the place described by Christians for whom it is a holy land and ultimate stage for the second coming of the Messiah. These eight books concern themselves with discontented Israelis who live in a country in which almost every facet of life is out of balance. They reflect a nation ill at ease with itself, floundering in seemingly insoluble contradictions.

Granted statehood in 1948, Israel was seen as ending the torments inherent in centuries of exile. Israel was to be a safe haven for Jews, no matter their country of origin. In the land of their biblical ancestors, Jews would realize their full potential without the fear and reality of persecution. Inhabiting their own space, these new Israelis would develop into strong, active, fully functioning human beings. The country, though Jewish, would be free from the strictures and inhibitions European Jews endured in enclosed communities that insisted on adherence to strict Jewish religious law. Israel was to be a secular democracy, not one inhabited by weak-bodied religious scholars like those who suffered mass humiliation and death in the Holocaust. In such institutions as the *kibbutz*, communal life in the new nation was touted as a sure means of insuring confident, fearless children and healthy, happy adults.

The actual term "holy land" (in Hebrew *eretz ha kadosh*) is not cited in Hebrew scripture. *Ideas* of holiness, however, permeate the text. The notion of that which is holy refers largely to the nature of God, to the quality of this deity's relationship to the people of Israel, and to those obligations expected if the Israelites are to fulfill their role as a special people chosen by their God for certain privileges. The Hebrew word for holy—*kadosh*—connotes that which is set apart for a special purpose.

Over time, however, the phrase "holy land" increasingly was used as descriptor for that part of the Middle East thought to be the locus of sites deemed sacred by the three Abrahamic religions—Judaism, Christianity, and Islam. The term marks out an exceptional space, one in which specific sites are believed to be the locus of events related to divinely inspired foundation stories of these three religions. A reliance on biblical text as justification for key elements of Israel's foundation insists that since the time of Abraham, there has been a continuous Jewish presence in Israel. This notion is challenged, however, by revisionist Israeli historians who argue that ancient narratives have been changed to suit contemporary narrators. Furthermore, pointing out that Israel still has no fixed borders, Idith Zertal (2005) writes, "The deliberate transience of the political border and the blurred spheres around it as established by Israel's governments also left ample space for the emergence of a mythology of the true, promised, sacred 'other' border. . ." (185). No agreement regarding the fundamental question as to which physical borders actually delineate the putative holy land of Israel has yet been made. The possibility of an ever-elusive holiness without boundaries beckons, an impossible mirage continually dissolving.

Threads relating to notions of holiness are woven throughout foundational Zionist narratives, though the preponderance of this quality varies in both centrality and potency. Often the idea was invoked for purely utilitarian, political reasons. For early Zionists, the notion of holiness was infinitely less important than the idea of ethnic national autonomy. However, in contemporary common parlance, the term "holy land" is continually used interchangeably with Israel. Leaving aside the reality that there are other lands deemed holy by other religions, the idea of Israel as a sacred place stems from an insistence by Jewish, Muslim, and Christian religionists that this particular place is unquestionably exceptional as guaranteed in the Hebrew Bible, the subsequent New Testament, and the Koran. In Bethlehem, the graves of Abraham and Sarah are not metaphorical resting grounds. Jews are told that they contain the actual tomb of this founding patriarch and his wife, and

Christians locate Christ's actual birthplace there. The Dome of the Rock is one of Islam's most holy sites.

Cities and sites are not seen as symbols; they are held to be contemporary continuations of sacred ancient history. Israel is not a modern nation-state subject to conflicts and impelled by a need to compromise, to struggle towards reconciling opposing desires. It is exempt from critique because it is a holy land deriving its legitimacy from God. Criticism is muted or silenced in the face of divine validity. Notions of national exceptionalism as ordained by heavenly decree weave a curtain that obscures everyday discontent, masking the need to confront the unease burgeoning on so-called holy soil.

The dominant narrative of modern-day Israeli apologists is challenged by that country's artists. If artists are any good, they are inherently subversive. Their gaze leads to new ways of perceiving accepted truths. The writers in this study undermine notions of an idealized Israel, inviting readers to reconsider ingrained perspectives. Three of the writers are women, and one is male. Israel's women writers are moving out of the margins, challenging the hegemony of male-dominated Israeli prose. Outsiders to the narratives that shape many stories Israelis tell themselves, they challenge basic aspects of Israel's masculinized culture. As they describe *their* Israel, Govrin, Castel-Bloom and Shalev are vital forces in reshaping its discourse.

These four particular authors were chosen partially because they are marginal; the view from the side often has far more interesting vistas than the gaze from the middle. All of these writers deserve wider recognition. They are bold, original, and readable for the sheer imagination of their invented worlds. Each of them challenges conventional wisdom on such issues as the Holocaust, religion, and the nature of family. None of them grants Israel special status as a holy land. The country they inhabit is an all-too-recognizable modern nation, with ills reflecting a twenty-first-century zeitgeist. Informed by an implicit understanding of an often-romanticized Zionist vision, each book is merciless in demonstrating that today's Israeli lives in a world far different from the special place described in founding narratives.

Each writer informs the other, and there are links between texts. Whether the issue under consideration is the Holocaust as it is for Kaniuk, the nature of the Jewish God and the role of women as with Govrin, the absurdity of Israeli institutions as portrayed by Castel-Bloom, or the crumbling of domestic life as with Shalev, each book adds to a portrait of contemporary cultural malaise. The term "Ashkenazi Jewish Israeli" is an apt descriptor of the works' subjects as these novels all take place in the context of a fictional universe peopled almost exclusively by Israeli Jews of European descent, so-called Ashkenazi Jews. In none of these books do Arab Jews, let alone Arabs, play a major role. There is a glancing reference to a Palestinian Arab lover in one book, and a lover in another is an Arab Jew. There are allusions to the

existence of non-Jewish Israelis, but the references are faint and the characters perfunctory.

Without dwelling on the presence of this absence, it is important to note
it. Approximately twenty percent of Israel's current population are non-Jewish Arabs, and significant numbers of Jews have Arab origins. Israeli writers
and intellectuals who are not European Jews struggle to be counted as equals
as they challenge the dominance of Ashkenazi Jews in the world of letters as
in almost all other domains. But it is no exaggeration to say that at this
juncture, it is the Ashkenazi Israeli experience that gets most of the attention—and the publishers and translators who make works available.

While this book is concerned with Israel, it is not directly about Judaism,
nor about Jews for whom the religious aspect of their identity is foremost.
The overarching issue tying these books together attempts to address the
questions, "What do these books describe about the contemporary Israeli
experience that normally lies unexposed or suppressed?" and "What does this
fiction tell readers about the psycho-subjective costs of living in such a riven
place?" This book challenges readers to look beyond religious or political
rhetoric to a place where contemporary people deal with existential issues
and quotidian miseries in a nation-state which defines itself as Jewish.

Implicit in all these books are the deeply entrenched terrors that have
marked the history of the people called Jews, a minority culture nearly annihilated over the centuries. Concerns revolve around the fear and very real
threat of disappearance through external force or via assimilation; the tension
between preserving ancient customs and the pull of the majority culture's
inviting possibilities; challenges to the idea that holding on to a specific
geographically bounded place is the only way to ensure survival no matter
that others claim that same space; the confusion that arises as parochial
concerns do battle with larger, more cosmopolitan issues; tensions between
religiosity and secularism. Aspects of these preoccupations torment the fictive characters in this imagined Israel. But like all good art, these novels have
universal relevance. A reader may put aside these readings and parse the
books through the lens of their particular concerns. Meeting these characters
and hearing their stories will do what all good art does: amaze and delight,
subvert and inform.

It is certain that Israeli culture and society will change over time. How it
will do so is very much in doubt. Just now, the country has taken a sharp turn
towards the political Right. Fundamentalist religious settlers exert an ever
more powerful influence on the direction of public policy, and there is talk of
preemptive strikes against a near neighbor. Official rhetoric suggests support
for a two-state solution, but the government's actions point to an unwilling-
ness to implement measures that could realistically lead to such a resolution.
Even once generally agreed-upon 1967 borders as boundaries for two states
are being questioned. Domestic issues such as the consequences of a lopsided

economy, concerns around a dwindling water supply, and the question of what to do with an influx of refugees from war-torn parts of Africa are markers of discordant days. Tumultuous times continue unabated, and Israeli artists and writers will continue to reflect upon the consequences of troubling social realities. Those who read their fiction will continue turning to them for insight in the search to understand Israel in all its cultural complexities.

Increasingly, core assumptions of founding Zionist discourse are being challenged, as within Israel debate about the nation's mission and purpose grows. In some quarters, the concept of Zionism itself is questioned, both as to its original intent and its current (mis)use to justify prevailing practices. Some challengers refer to themselves as post-Zionists, arguing that "maps of meaning provided by Zionism are simply no longer adequate" and "the problems that beset Israel . . . will only be settled when viable alternatives are found to the dominant Zionist dialogue" (Silberstein, 1999, 2-4). Whatever terms are used to frame the discourse, these novels reflect a long journey away from founding ideals of the State. The artists in this study, crucial voices in a post-Zionist Israeli dialogue, offer compelling portraits of how far contemporary Israel has traveled from the optimistic assumptions that informed the early life of the country.

The Israeli soul reflected in the fictive worlds of Yoram Kaniuk, Michael Govrin, Orly Castel-Bloom, and Zeruya Shalev is in peril. These artists have an intuitive sense of prevailing fragility, reflecting shared concerns about societal and individual disorder. Differing in content and style, there is one overarching link that may be discerned amongst all the novels: the preponderance of shame as a fundamental malaise afflicting everyone and everything.

Shame can be defined as "an experience of the self as diminished before another and . . . visible to another," (Miller, 1985, 32-33) or as "a violation of expectation, (of incongruity between expectation and outcome) resulting in a shattering of trust in oneself, even in one's own body—and in the world one has known" (Lynd, 1999, 46). The fictional characters in these works demonstrate that "shattering of trust in one's own body." Almost every person feels profoundly diminished, fundamentally damaged, ill at ease with themselves. Often this grave discomfort expresses itself in physical incapacity and illness, and other times it surfaces in an emotional or mental state—or in a combination of any or all of these manifestations. Almost no one feels that he or she is behaving in a manner worthy of respect, either from self or others. There is little or no trust in a larger world as the exterior plane is seen as a source of judgment and wounding. This deep sense of shame is evidence of an overall unease saturating the space these characters inhabit.

The bodies of characters are sources of ongoing betrayal. Physical selves are sites of profound disease, often literal embodiments of stultifying shame. In Govrin's novel *The Name,* Amalia is continually trying to atone for her sexuality and ultimately destroys herself in a final attempt to evade feelings of shame about her sexual misdeeds. In Kaniuk's *Adam Resurrected*, the title character becomes an animal as he is visited again and again by memories of unspeakably shaming physical degradation. Shalev's fictive Ari is sterile, and the character Na'ama sees her body as ugly and disgusting, something no man would want. Na'ama's husband Udi experiences paralysis and hysterical blindness. *Dolly City*'s Dolly continually disfigures bodies, literally slicing into them in a mad attempt to reorder the world. In *Snapshots*, Ilana's promiscuity is an attempt to sublimate shame through compulsive sexual activity. There is great variety in how bodies are sites of torment. But repeatedly, the physical self is deformed as individuals experience lives riven by ignominy.

Beyond individual struggles with shame as an imposing emotional presence, there are societal implications. An overarching sense of shame may be seen as playing out in Israeli culture as part of the dark legacy of the Holocaust. The historian Jacqueline Rose argues that shame and its unbearable weight leads Israelis to their retributive acts against Palestinians. Fundamentally, she suggests, it is almost impossible to bear the pain of the Holocaust. Yet the constantly evoked memory of this pain has become a central affirming principle for the existence of the state of Israel. Rose (2005) writes, "when suffering becomes an identity, it has to turn cruel in order to be able to bear, or live with itself" (115). It is not only the unspeakable events of the Holocaust itself that are unbearable. The shame it engenders is warping the nation's soul. Inability to directly confront the humiliations and agony of this catastrophe drives the resultant shame underground. What surfaces is cruelty to the Palestinian Other and a remorseless insistence that such treatment is justified. "[S]omething horrific becomes psychically intolerable [and it must]—*at one and the same time*—to be repeated and denied" (146).

Indescribable catastrophe is never totally absent in any of these books. The Holocaust is most directly referenced in Kaniuk's *Adam Resurrected*, which tells the story of Adam's terrible life in a concentration camp, and thus makes the Holocaust a central character. In *His Daughter*, much of what occurs is understandable only if we remember that the general's ex-wife is a Holocaust survivor. The general continually struggles to understand what this means for him as an Israeli, and for their daughter who reflects both cultures. Kaniuk's characters are best understood as individuals whose lives are marked by the Holocaust, their motivations growing directly out of the trauma that continues to live inside them. The result is an ongoing cycle with victims taking on the role of tormentors. This psychological wreckage is passed from one generation to the next, and often results in mental derangement that shatters relationships both with self and others. In Israel, the pernicious effects of the Holocaust continue to poison.

Orly Castel-Bloom's satire offers a way out of despair in the face of entrenched institutional, individual, and national stupidity. She satirizes the foolish ways Israeli government, media, medicine, and business institutions respond to social and individual ills. Her writing is hilarious and her characters outrageous. Castel-Bloom bears favorable comparison to Jonathan Swift, and there are intriguing parallels between postcolonial contemporary Israel and eighteenth-century Ireland. The author mocks some of the most deeply held beliefs that underlie the view of Israel as a land beyond reproach where anything it does, no matter how crazy or destructive, is not to be challenged. Castel-Bloom creates lunatic situations featuring imaginatively deranged individuals in a science fiction-like Israeli context. Her portrait of people running amuck is uproariously funny as well as deeply infuriating.

God and text are central in the works of Michal Govrin, along with a focus on ways in which male religiosity may destroy a woman's spirituality. Jews' reverence for the written word has its roots in ancient study. The Hebrew Bible and its various commentaries still serve as the basis for many of the ways Jews formulate their world-view, even when this foundation is not explicitly acknowledged. Religious Zionist claims to Israel rest on the notion that this particular piece of land was divinely given to the Jews. The Jewish notion of God is multiple and varied, and runs the gamut from nuanced symbol to doctrinaire rigidity. Govrin is masterful at writing about individuals for whom the notion of God is at the heart of life and death choices. Her characters struggle to live as righteous Jews based on their understanding of how biblical text represents such notions as divinity and sin. Searching for a hallowed connection is ultimately corrosive for her fictive women, and Govrin invites us to consider how concepts of holiness can play out in life-destroying ways in today's Israeli culture.

Zeruya Shalev's domestically oriented novels examine Jews and their bodies, particularly in relation to concepts around sexuality. Early Zionist myths articulated a notion of the "new Jew" who would be free in body as well as in spirit. As the founding myths of Zionism disintegrate under modern-day pressures, even the most personal concerns are impacted. Shalev creates portraits of disintegrating domestic worlds that mirror larger facts of chaos in Israel. Her characters are sexually promiscuous and emotionally disturbed. The world they inhabit offers little in the way of solace or clarity. Familial and gender roles are confused as men and women confront the fact that new realities demand changed definitions of male and female, husband and wife, parent and child. Shalev's characters are deformed by their inability to create relationships that break from the past in order to exist meaningfully in the present.

These books exist in a historical context, reflecting a time and place— early twenty-first century Israel—where people are struggling with a particular set of issues. Over time, and depending on what happens, some of these issues will fade from the foreground. Founding Zionist myths and their contemporary manifestations will be augmented by other narratives. Suggesting an alternative to outdated national narratives is one of the invaluable functions of these literary creations. Examining, for example, how the Holocaust is used to grant legitimacy to some of Israel's destructive actions implies absolutely no denial of this catastrophe. Rather, confronting the implications of this narrative encourages an understanding of how the past can warp as well as inspire. Reframing the plots of Israel's sustaining stories is an extremely painful but essential step towards conceptualizing new ways of directing the country's energy.

Considering how these authors challenge a national self-image built on outmoded perceptions is not so much to experience hope as to begin the painful process of acknowledging despair. Their literature is a light unto the nation, and to those outside the nation for whom Israel is a profoundly important entity. Kaniuk, Govrin, Shalev, and Castel-Bloom's brilliant portraits of Israeli life today suggest alternatives to current self-deluding stories that seek to deny that there is much in Israel seriously in need of repair. Entering their fictive worlds may help to encourage the painful process of redemption, both amongst Israelis and those who support the nation's best hopes for itself.

Chapter One

The Ongoing Shadow Of The Holocaust

Yoram Kaniuk

Now I am become Death, the destroyer of worlds.
(Bhagavad Gita, verse 32)

To begin to make sense of the contemporary Jewish psyche as it functions in the world in general and Israel in particular, it is essential to understand the Holocaust in the formation of Jewish identity. The singular event lives on, a specter stalking the interior landscape of Jews worldwide. Its pernicious impact on a Jewish worldview is monumental, whether or not Jews are consciously alert to its demonic presence. While memories of the Holocaust are particularly vivid for Jews over fifty years of age, younger generations are enjoined never to forget this catastrophe and to be continuously on-guard for signs of a recurrence.

The narrative of the Holocaust is passed from generation to generation, casting its shadow such that Jews feel fundamentally unsafe in the world. Extracting a continuous toll of psychic misery, the catastrophe haunts Jewish communal life in Israel and beyond. Much attention is devoted to keeping the devastating enterprise alive in memory. There are Holocaust museums throughout the world, including one in Washington, D.C., which has had over fifty million visitors since its 1993 opening.

Each year, thousands of teenagers from all over the world take part in a March of the Living, walking just under two miles from Auschwitz to Birkenau, the largest concentration camp complex built by the Nazis. They are taught about the Holocaust and enjoined to understand its primary role in the formation of Jewish identity.[1]

In the national narratives Israelis tell themselves and their children, the Holocaust is the *ur* story, the insistent reference point for a nation ever alert and ready to fight for its life. The dark shadow of the Holocaust (referred to in Hebrew as the *Shoah*) significantly influences how Israel and its supporters worldwide respond to the situation in the Middle East today. An internalized terror that mass destruction will happen again without constant vigilance distorts public policy decisions. Most crucially, this catastrophe has taken on mythic characteristics. A key component in framing the story of Zionism, it is often invoked to justify Israel's bellicose acts in the name of ensuring that "never again" will Jews be slaughtered en masse.

Avraham Burg (2008), former speaker of the Israeli Knesset, has detailed the overwhelming power this catastrophe exacts on Israelis' interior lives. The title of his book, *The Holocaust Is Over; We Must Rise from Its Ashes*, sums up his impassioned argument that Israel is endangering its very soul by using the Holocaust to justify acts of violence and repression against others and to feed a culture of fear and paranoia. Writing that ". . . the *Shoah* is the main generator that feeds the mentalities of confrontation and catastrophic Zionism," (15), Burg argues for the need to break the vicious cycle which obsessive fear of another Holocaust engenders.

Idith Zertal (2005), an Israeli historian, also maintains that the Holocaust dangerously distorts contemporary Israel's perspective. She insists that "Israel's collective memory of death and trauma [is] . . . processed, coded and put to use in Israel's public space, particularly in the half-century . . . since the destruction of European Jewry" (1). Israel perceives itself "as a trauma-community, a 'victim community,' one which . . . recounts itself through the unifying memory of catastrophes, suffering, and victimization" (2). Furthermore,

> [W]hen transformed by the religious imagination into myth, the experience of victimization can confer a kind of holiness and power upon the victim. In stories constructed around disaster and destruction, the victim is always both victim and victor, always destroyed but always reborn in a form that overcomes the victimizer. The chief beneficiary of that empowerment . . . is the community . . . as the historical body whose very existence preserves and relives the moment of degradation and transfiguration . . . Israeli society has defined itself in relation to the Holocaust. (2-3)

Zertal's comments pull no punches; she is damning in her bold assessment of the ongoing power of the Holocaust in her country's psyche, a catastrophe that has assumed the status of defining myth. Seeing itself as a victim community, Israel grants itself permission to proceed as it sees fit in matters of defense. Seeking to barricade itself from the role of victim, bulwarks are created against any repeat of the suffering once inflicted upon the Jewish people. A stated fear of catastrophe grants legitimacy to whatever acts are deemed necessary to avenge the past and prevent its recurrence. The phrase "never again" is repeatedly invoked, entering the world's vocabulary as a refrain which has become code for signaling support of actions deemed essential to defend Israeli policy decisions. United States President Obama (2012) invoked the words on a day set aside as Holocaust Remembrance Day remarking, "Together with the State of Israel, and all our friends around the world, we dedicate ourselves to giving meaning to those powerful words: 'Never Forget. Never Again.'"

A person like myself is caught in a tangle of responses. Like many people, I have read myriad descriptions of the Holocaust, and am continually reminded of it as a member of the Jewish community. I myself did not lose family members to this catastrophe. My ancestry is largely Russian, and their exodus was from Czarist Russia and not from Nazi Germany. But for myself as for many Jews, the Holocaust carries a significant meta-meaning that must be factored in any attempt to parse out key elements of Jewish identity. The scale, the sadistic cruelty and the unspeakable acts of degradation are nearly impossible to take in. Six million Jews were murdered, leaving a gaping hole which will never close over. Furthermore, anti-semitism remains ever present; nothing is able to rid the world of its evil. Groups of people will always find reasons to hate the Jews.

Nevertheless, I wish to articulate a set of responses which does not rely on the Holocaust as a core aspect of Jewish identity to justify ongoing fear and a persistent hypervigilance to perceived threats. Attempting to navigate the tension between memory and forgetting and to comprehend more fully the deadly grip of this singular catastrophe, I turn to Yoram Kaniuk. His two novels, *Adam Resurrected* and *His Daughter*, encapsulate the terrible experience of the Holocaust and help suggest how the events of that time continue to poison the ability of Jews to think beyond that monumental tragedy. Both novels are peopled by characters whose lives have been disfigured by what happened in the death camps, even though they live now in Israel which was to be the land of deliverance. It is useful to grapple with Kaniuk because he helps to clarify, with startling profundity, the source of so much pain and the near-impossible difficulty in healing old yet still suppurating wounds.

Kaniuk's characters are broken and full of anguish, unredeemed and tormented. They make love, give birth, carry on living. But they cannot rid themselves of the wounded beast within. And the demon lives on as children are enshrouded in their parents' darkness. The writer Eva Hoffman (2004), herself a survivor of Polish devastation, writes of this event as "the heavy ground of being, the natural condition to which the world tend[s]" (4). For Hoffman, "The Holocaust [became] . . . a kind of story about the basic elements and shape of the world, a childish mythos or fable" (15).

Surely she who was so close to the actual event has the right to remind Jews that in seeing the Holocaust as the basis for much of our worldview, we construct systems of belief which move us towards giving this unspeakable tragedy the power of legend. Through Kaniuk's powerful prose, one begins to comprehend the efficacy of the mythos as well as some of the realities of the Holocaust. Mythic aspects of the catastrophe have strengthened over time, enlarging the experience into something almost otherworldly in its ghastly authority. The Holocaust might almost be viewed as a negative theology, a belief system with a great darkness at its heart.

To argue that the Holocaust has become a myth-like foundation story is in no conceivable way to suggest it did not happen. This discussion does not hint at such a blasphemy. But it does make the case that the Holocaust's very enormity has transformed the tragedy into something superhuman, shaping itself into a larger-than-life narrative which wields enormous power in formulating thought and emotion.

There is understandable resistance to the notion that the Holocaust has taken on mythic elements, as this may be taken as a diminution of this unutterable catastrophe. Furthermore, suggesting that the mythologizing of the Holocaust has turned it into a less than noble force in determining contemporary actions can lead to bitter, defensive resistance as people dig in their heels to reinforce the strength of a master story. Challenging narratives that shape the way a community defines itself can marshal persons to literally defend to the death their collective set of stories. But if myth is understood in its sense of an almost supernatural tale that shapes a worldview, perhaps such a construct can help clarify how foundation stories may function as an impediment to clearheaded thinking.

This includes myths that are based on indisputably real events of an enormous and terrible nature, like the Holocaust. Perhaps it is only through fiction created by a masterful writer like Yoram Kaniuk that one can even begin to contend with the negative impact of this embedded narrative. Kaniuk helps deconstruct Holocaust mythology as he fabricates stories which illuminate the darkness the *Shoah* continues to engender. He tells stories about The Story, making it accessible and open to reexamination.

THE MASK OF MADNESS (*ADAM RESURRECTED*)

Adam Resurrected is a riveting account of madness, a raw and brilliant exposé into the mind of a man driven insane by his experience in one of the German death camps. There is no restraint in the narrative. Adam Stein's story as related in the third person in *Adam Resurrected* is a nonstop encounter with anguish, told with a force that invites the reader to cry out in the presence of such profound pain. Reading it is to be stunned at the power of words to re-create the impossible. In this novel, Kaniuk (1971) demonstrates how a work of fiction can evoke the horrible reality of a major historic event by writing about it through the experience of one lone invented individual.

The novel unflinchingly examines the interior life of one man who survived debasement and near-death at the hands of the Nazis only to annihilate himself through madness. Losing his mind is the only way Adam Stein can cope with what happened to him in a death camp. When he does recover his sanity, he loses an essential part of himself. Obliterating the past may be the only way to survive it, but Adam also feels that "Sanity is pleasant, calm, amusing, but it lacks greatness, it lacks true joy as well as the awful sorrow which slashes the heart" (368-69). It may be that the memory of sorrow works similarly in the collective Jewish psyche; to relinquish the agony of the past is to lose a sense of greatness in the moment. But the greatness that comes from awful sorrow may lead to actions better left undone. The agonies of remembered humiliation may lead to inflicting that same state upon others.

We first meet Adam in a Tel Aviv pension run by the lovely German-born Jew, Ruth, the lover he tries to strangle in a fit of madness. As a consequence, he is taken off to an asylum in the Israeli desert town of Arad, where he has twice before been incarcerated. Ruth reluctantly sees him off. In spite of Adam's attack on her and despite the fact that he is often wildly erratic, she has also found in him a thoughtful, attentive lover. In addition, he is a companion with whom to share common loves in music, food, and wine.

It is Ruth-as-German that is at the heart of Adam's attraction. The lovers share past lives as inhabitants of that nation. In the presence of his lover, he is back in his beloved Berlin. For Adam, "Ruthie's German and her lovely body . . . poured into him the peaceful feeling that a child has on returning home" (8). "The Berlin of his youth was right here, and more alive here than there" (10). In fact, the novel ends with Adam's return to Ruth's domicile. Adam finds a measure of contentment in coming back to a countrywoman who reunites him with associations to the place wherein he suffered near total destruction. Throughout the novel, Adam will reencounter figures from Germany who have become embedded in his psychic landscape. There is no way he can escape these companions; even the camp commandment resides inside him waiting to be rediscovered in Israel. Inside mad, alive, conflicted, absurd, Israeli citizen Adam is a proud son of Germany.

The irony of Germany as home is deliberate. It is in the *idea* of Germany, not the *reality* of Israel, that Adam finds solace. Though the novel ends on a somewhat upbeat note with Adam circling back to the familiar comfort of Germany as embodied in Ruth, this in no way makes his journey any less harrowing. The novel is a chronicle of Adam's degradation in one of the concentration camps, an account of how his madness plays out in himself and in his fellow inmates in the Israeli Institute for Rehabilitation and Therapy. It is also a bitter and sometimes humorous commentary on such things as American Jewish money in Israel, the role and buffoonery of psychiatrists who cannot truly understand madness, and the idea that God may or may not be crazy.

Adam's own story is simple and it is terrible. He was a hugely successful circus clown and violinist in Berlin, renowned for his ability to amuse and delight. He is taken to one of the concentration camps, and under the aegis of the camp's commander is spared from the gas chambers in return for clowning for the inmates as they are taken off to die. "In order that [the inmates] might die in peace, he [the camp commandant] grabbed the great clown Adam and authorized him to survive. . . . Nothing disturbed Commandant Klein as much as the dread that they might die screaming. . . . Therefore . . . Stein played and joked" (107).

He performs brilliantly, assuaging inmates' fears: "His whole purpose was to blot out the fear of death . . . Germany's greatest clown would be right up front clowning. After all, if such a person were around, things couldn't be so bad" (127). Adam has convinced himself that his terrible work in fact has a kind of meaning; it offers solace to those soon to perish. Having found a reason to justify his terrible role, Adam functions as a musical clown under the commandant's sinister, watchful eye.

And then one day he performs as his wife Gretchen and their daughter Lotta pass in front of him on their way to extinction. "So Adam didn't address his wife or child, and to the very end they walked with trust and peace in their hearts" (127). He tries to deny this, to save "himself from the shame which was his greatest fear, the shame of guilt" (127). But he cannot rid himself of this shameful guilt, and his memories of clowning before his soon to be slain wife and child. He carries all of this with him when he moves to Israel. There he loses his mind and succumbs to debilitating attacks both physical and mental. Again and again, Adam recalls joking and playing music so Jews would walk calmly to their destruction and not disturb the commandant with needless noise. Repeatedly he remembers seeing his family off to be gassed. These recurring images refuse to dim. Only debilitating fits temporarily blot out the ghastly recollections.

This central trope is difficult enough to take in, but there are other incidents in the book that are almost unbearable. A central brilliance of *Adam Resurrected* is Kaniuk's ability to write about the most extreme darkness in ways that make it possible to begin to imagine the unimaginable. In one scene, Adam describes competing for food with the commandant's dog Rex as they both gobble what is in the bowls on the floor: "On all fours [Adam] crawled over to Rex [the commandant's dog], rubbed against him, nose to nose. . . . The two of [them], on all fours, used to tear the meat off the bones" (81). This signal image of human degraded into animal is a summation of countless incidents of perversity. Kaniuk unerringly finds ways to describe the indescribable.

The master-dog relationship plays out repeatedly and is one of the central metaphors underscoring the links between master and slave, victor and victim, conqueror and conquered, Jew and German. To be a dog is to be a less than human beast. All the major characters in *Adam Resurrected* take their turns being dog and being master. Watching these roles shift is to witness a spectacle in which the partners are locked into a dreadful dance of power and submission, top dog and underdog, humiliator and humiliated taking turns.

The initial master-dog connection is between Adam and the camp commander. In the death camp, Adam is Commandant Klein's pet. He is fed, protected, defined within this relationship. After the war, Adam repeatedly visits the commandant who is living in disgrace in postwar Berlin and brings him food and money. Now it is Adam who is in charge, master to his former protector. In the asylum where he is confined, Adam is the master and has his own "dog" in the person of a young boy who is a fellow inmate. With the head nurse Jenny, Adam returns to the role of dog, dependent on someone else for food, grooming and protection. On and on it goes, individuals playing out an anguished struggle to vanquish Other and emerge victorious. It would seem that only in another's suffering is any sense of validation to be found.

While Adam's death camp experiences and his madness are central, *Adam Resurrected* may lead us beyond that initial horror into a consideration of the implications of that singular tragedy for contemporary Israel. Kaniuk demonstrates through his characters' lives how the Holocaust warps people. In some cases, it is a firsthand devastation. Others were not physically present yet bear the catastrophe's psychic burdens. The fallout manifests itself in the Israel of today, impacting individual and collective souls as the Holocaust is invoked to justify key elements of Israeli policy. A representative quote by the Israeli Defense Force Chief of the General Staff (2011) encapsulates the centrality of the *Shoah*: "As in every year, we return to a place of personal connection to the horrors of the Holocaust. . . . We stand here . . . the commanders of the Israel Defense Forces, promising that we, as an army, as a country and a nation will never forget the horrors of the Holocaust." In evoking the unspeakable degradations of the Holocaust through the experiences of one man, Kaniuk helps us understand beyond the shadow of a doubt why its influence on Israeli policy in particular and Jewish thought in general is so unrelentingly powerful.

But *Adam Resurrected* works to subvert the view that having suffered immeasurably makes it acceptable to inflict suffering in return. The asylum, located on the edge of the desert, is a self-contained universe in which it's difficult to tell who is crazy and who is not. Clearly, the inmates are peculiar critters whose speech, dress, and actions are aberrant. But what is one to make of Jenny, the head nurse and Adam's lover? Jenny is twenty-five years old, beautiful, and cold. The inmates are "scared stiff of her, and only her. . . . Marble. Coldness. Hate" (24). But "For the past two months she has been praying for [Adam's] return" (24).

Her passion for Adam is intense and highly sexual. Their lovemaking is passionately unreserved: "he joins her to him and with joy she takes his sex in her hand . . . and kisses him, crying" (158). Jenny longs for Adam when he is not around. She will do anything for him, from the most elemental grooming to overlooking his rule breaking, however egregious that may be. But she is also a martinet, thin-lipped and strict with the inmates. She insists on order, on things being done in the right way, and will tolerate no deviation from the rules she has laid down. In a scene interrupting the inmates engaged in knitting, Jenny's all-seeing power is portrayed: "Her arm outstretched . . . her eyes everywhere . . . the fear. . . . Nothing escapes the lighthouse sweep of her vision" (112).

Jenny is clearly disturbed in ways that demonstrate how tightly interwoven are seeming opposites. We are told that "whenever he [Adam] is released from the Institute . . . she sinks into a lethargy, as though she herself were dying . . . the moment he is back . . . she revives like spring. . . . She knows she is in love not merely with his life . . . but also with the death implicit in every step of his. . . . If not for the fact of death, she would fear life" (71). It is a distressing reality that neither health nor release is what Nurse Jenny wants for Adam, for the other inmates, for herself. What she wants is a connection to extinction, to the fact of death, and to control those who are close to some kind of dying. She dwells amidst ongoing death since the vast majority of the asylum inmates are Holocaust survivors stalked by constant memories of genocide. And she lives in a time and a place where conflict has become a fact of everyday life. This supposed nurse/healer prefers the shadows to existence in a less fraught world.

Most disturbing is the thread linking Jenny to other tyrants, even to Hitler. "Jenny loves Adam the way she loves inflexible commandments. . . . [Adam] wanted to say that Commandant Klein and she, despite obvious differences, were quite alike" (110). "In awe of her ability to be simultaneously human and bestial . . . he wants to shout: *Heil, Hitler!*" (112-13). In Adam's eyes, her relationship to the incarcerated inmates in the Institute for Rehabilitation and Therapy and to him is not dissimilar to the human interactions dictated by Hitler and his cohorts. In fact, Adam sometimes sees her as the detested tyrant himself. Like the Nazis and their leader, she is bestial. Like them, she wants above all to control.

Only with Adam would Jenny *appear* to be someone different, a person soft and loving. Their relationship, intensely sexual, is suffused with traits recognizable in torrid love affairs of all kinds. But, and this is a large and crucial "but," Adam thinks of himself as a dog. When he was in the death camp, he was a dog. Now that he is in the asylum, he is still a dog. But this time, he is Jenny's dog. We are stunned as we recognize that the dog-master dynamic is intrinsic to their relationship. Adam has exchanged his master Commandant Klein for that of his master Jenny. "He honored her because, as a dog eating from Commandant Klein's dog bowl, he had learned to respect the whip and pay homage to the victor . . . Jenny was an inspiration to him . . . Jenny represented the race of conquerors" (112). In her authoritative role as nurse in this asylum, Jenny represents the State for she runs an institution which is part of the national infrastructure. For Adam, her dog, she is part of a new race of not-so-admirable victors.

As Commandant Klein's dog, Adam clowned for the Jews on their way to the ovens. As Jenny's dog, he performs sexually. With both masters, his humanity is annihilated as Adam subsumes himself to the dictates of a malevolent other. Part of Adam's resurrection is his dawning understanding of the sickness inherent in his relationship with Jenny. She is deeply dismayed when Adam is restored to himself as a functional human being for she wishes him to remain a patient, maimed and in need of treatment. After his release, in a first-person postscript acknowledging the nature of their bond, Adam writes:

> In the Institute for Rehabilitation and Therapy there never was such a marvelous lunatic as Jenny. . . . I've been out of the Institute for a whole year now and she still hasn't visited me. My letters she doesn't answer . . . though week after week I receive letters addressed to Adam Stein, Dog, Inc., these letters are not for *me*. They are for the Adam Stein she knew at the Institute. *Me* she refuses to acknowledge. . . . She loved only one man in her life, and that man I murdered. The moment I recovered, Adam Stein was buried. Jenny is still in mourning for him. (359-60)

The power of these observations lies in their ability to encapsulate resistance to healing, to change, to a shift in the status quo. They also point to the thin lines delineating boundaries between opposing traits. Fashioning Jenny, Kaniuk again melds opposites and suggests an ongoing connection between healer and destroyer, lover and enslaver, sanity and madness. Disease and disorder seduce Nurse Jenny; health and wholeness are scorned. Adam's equation of Israeli Jenny with Hitler and with the concentration camp commander invite us to consider that while the players may alter over time, a malevolent mission may continue—this time in Israel itself. Healed at last, Adam identifies with telling accuracy the real lunatic now: Nurse Jenny.

Scenes incorporating extended images of dog/animal and man/Adam provide vivid insights into relationships twisted by various power dynamics and reflect imbalances in the larger culture. Adam himself has his own dog whom he encounters during one of his wanderings through the halls of the asylum. Hearing barking sounds as he listens through a door, "The frightened animal's growls are intelligible to him. If he wanted to, Adam could answer back, growl for growl" (360). We know without being told that it's a human making these noises, not a dog. We know because Kaniuk has drawn us so completely into the world of Adam—performer, lover, near-murderer, charismatic inmate amongst inmates, but above all dog—that Dog Adam has now found a dog of his own. The relationship that unfolds between Adam and the dog/boy is the hopeful part of this difficult story, and it is Adam's healing of the boy that marks his own resurrection.

The bonding between them and the salvation of each unfolds slowly, with many setbacks. At various times, Adam hates the boy. For his part, the boy often feels abandoned by Adam and lives in terror that Adam will leave him. The up and down relationship is marked most notably by Adam's periodic retreats into madness. But he persists in relating to the boy, and his instinct that the dog under the covering is a boy is confirmed: "The dog casts the sheet off his head . . . and shrinks into a corner. Shivering. Then Adam realizes that all along he knew what he now knows. . . . A child, a dog; a dog, a child. A child that is not a child, and a dog that is not a dog" (149).

It is almost unbearable to Adam, he who is both man and dog himself. We watch as "A tear forms in his eye. A tear of disappointment. A hunted animal is staring at Adam. . . . A child that is an animal. . . . And he, he knows neither what to give, nor what to say, nor how to rescue" (150). His disappointment is towards himself; after all, is it too much to ask of the dog/man that he rescue the dog/boy? Apparently, it is for "through the slit of his clenched teeth . . . he shoots out his words with the staccato rhythm of thunder: 'Listen, dog, don't dare depend on me. Don't rely on me . . . I am a broken reed. I will snap before your eyes'" (150).

Faced with acknowledging his own humanity through recognizing the dog/boy's humanness, Adam's first instinct is to escape back into madness. Stunned by a surge of genuine feeling, Adam is terrified. In spite of his apprehension, "Adam embraces the child . . . tears flow. . . . Adam . . . feels those tears . . . all of a sudden something terrible, something monstrous, becomes clear to him, something he no longer has any control over. He realizes that these tears are not the tears of an animal . . . the dog . . . is in fact a child". This is the most terrifying thing of all and "Adam is struck by terrific pains that split his back, that contort his body . . . he rises, bursts through the door, and escapes from the room" (221).

This is Adam's first attempt at retreat from the boy/dog, a return to the safety of an obliterating physical and mental agony. In fact, he snaps a few more times. In one of his fevered, broken states, he hallucinates as he spontaneously bleeds for no apparent reason:

> Adam sees himself. A child. A child. A young boy. A young boy becoming an
> adult. A young man. A man. A clown. A student. A philosopher. A violinist. A

joker. A comedian. A thinker. A charmer. A husband. A father. A dog. God. . . . Adam buckles, eyes ripped open, muddy, his brain a mixture of fog, his eyes a mixture of tears, Adam buckles and falls . . . hemorrhages, spits blood, screams. They tie him to a stretcher and carry him out. Four nurses bearing a hemorrhaging dog. (236-38)

But he does not disintegrate and he does not remain submerged in his torment. Most important, he does not abandon the boy. Released from the infirmary, "wearing his best suit," Adam goes to the dog/boy's room and asks "Do you know why I didn't come?" (242). Answering his own question, he replies, "The question is why I didn't die, not why I didn't come. . . . I didn't die because I wanted to come back and see you again . . . in order to see your face again, you, the dog . . . I came back" (243). And then the ultimate admission, the words coming out of a sorrowing and broken heart: " I love you, child" (246).

The poignancy of this writing, of its meaning, is nearly unbearable. Seeing into the soul of another, and stripping away the protective shell of his own dog-like sense of self, is too much for Adam. Fellow feeling is fraught with dangerous anguish. It is better to forgo even the most benign human stirrings (for how could one shrink from being loved by a boy who has come to adore you) than to experience dangerous eddies of emotion. Most dreadful is the beginning of human feeling for those who have become as dogs to us; once the Other is human in our eyes, we do not know what to do. Adam says, "In a world that lacks all meaning because it lacks the fear of death and has only the fear of life—yes, most people fear the wrong things—a dog is the height of meaning" (82). When a dog becomes a human, whether that dog is our own self or someone else, the resulting feelings may be close to intolerable. To experience the agony of recognizing self in other and giving up fear is to relinquish part of our links to death, even death on such a massive scale as that of the Holocaust.

What happens with Adam and the boy is a miracle of transformation, something transcendent arising out of near-total degradation. At first, the boy/man relationship mirrors that which Adam had with the death camp's Commandant Klein in which Adam was the dog. In the asylum, the boy is dog and Adam his deranged master (until Adam makes his monumental shift). A bitter irony stems from this role-playing taking place within an Israeli establishment. In this state asylum is to be found a re-creation of abasement, a reenactment of power run amuck and persons confined to crazy institutions not of their making. Situations of near inhuman deprivation are happening in Israel, which was to be a place of redemption. But Kaniuk shows us a site of profound disorder. Here is madness that blossoms as the line between man and dog, animal and beast, is confounded; a terrible derailment is taking place where there was to be salvation.

The asylum may be read as a sentinel safeguarding the power of the State, a place which admits of no reality outside itself. Nothing good exists beyond its walls. When a group of inmates go beyond the confines of the asylum into the desert, they nearly die: "the 'nation' leaves the courtyard of the synthetic sanctuary . . . and is swallowed by the darkness of the great desert that closes in on all sides . . . locusts marching into a wasteland" (290-91). Outside the walls of the fortress lies only oblivion, and those who seek to form a little band of brothers to breach the encircling stockade are as insects. They cannot exist outside that which both protects and imprisons them.

Reading Yoram Kaniuk is to begin to understand that the asylum dwellers, protected and imprisoned, demonstrate what still terrifies Jews on a visceral and almost genetic level today. This is what happened, they cry out, this is what our parents and grandparents and aunts and cousins and siblings went through. No matter what it takes, we shall not let it happen to us again. We will smite those who might smite us, and we will destroy if necessary those who might hurt us. We will control potential enemies, keeping them in a state of dependency. We will find large and small ways to make our enemies less than human. We ourselves have been mortally humiliated and never again shall this be so.

If there is any question about the connection that is often forged between captor and captured, victim and victimizer, torturer and tortured, Kaniuk makes it explicit when he writes of Adam's desert vision. The motley group of inmates who have walked out into the desert in search of God have become increasingly cold, thirsty, and frightened as night comes on. Adam goes off by himself, and "he believes . . . yes, *he* shall stand face to face with God, he believes it through and through. . . . And at that very moment he hears the Voice address him . . . *the voice of Commandant Klein*" (298) (Author's italics). The two speak, and Adam thinks, "Klein hasn't changed. . . . God crosses his legs and sits there. . . . They gaze at each other. Such a simple matter to be in God's presence!" (301). God in the desert is the commandant of the camp where Adam lived and nearly died. God is his German tormentor transformed into his Jehovah.

It's astonishing how Kaniuk makes the scene between Adam and Commandant Klein believable as both a deluded man's encounter with an imaginary supernatural being and also a meeting of two old comrades eternally linked by their shared past. God is an old friend, there when you least expect to see him. Adam tells Klein, "I love you. I know that you're a bastard, but I love you. We are both lost, we have both perished. . . . Our voices are the voices of ghosts. Jew to Jew, God to Son of God, man to father of man. You, my God, shall wait for me at the end of the road" (303).

Adam's tormentor has become his God, that transcendent force which provides meaning and direction. At the end of Adam's search lies his old master and tormentor, the camp commandant. And Adam loves him. Yes, he loves the one who fed him from a dog bowl on the floor. His torturer has become his deity, and his destroyer his savior and comrade. Together they have become a god of death, and Adam says, "Jewish history is over . . . or maybe it's just beginning. . . . We are living in a cemetery. There is nothing to rescue" (301).

Have we Jews come to worship that which almost destroyed us, that which was once abhorrent? Adam has become Klein, camp commandant; dog is one with hated master. What dark gods are we Jews invoking? But if we read Adam as a personification of the Jew nearly destroyed by the horrors visited upon him, and as we witness his torments after arrival in a supposed safe haven, we may begin to consider that doing evil to those who may visit malevolence upon us is the *likely* response. Emerging from profound degradation as a human being who does the right thing by others really makes no sense. Suffering indescribable humiliation does not inoculate against doing wrong towards others. It may, in fact, increase the desire to bury such humiliation under acts of aggression. The historian Jacqueline Rose (2005) writes "a people . . . who have been the object of violence are then faced with the dilemma of what to do with the internal debris of their own past" (145).

Perhaps, though, there is a beckoning light. After all, Adam was resurrected. And a god of death may also be interpreted as a deity of transformation. Adam began to feel again, loving and cherishing the boy. He left the asylum, this time for good. And he went back to Ruth, the woman he almost strangled, the lovely German Ruth. "When Ruthie spoke, he saw the mysterious beauty of an old book . . . a picture from the house of his parents . . . he heard the voice of his mother and Uncle Franz-Joseph and his father" (6). This is a relatively happy ending to a dark story, a reunion with the ghosts of beloved relatives in the recesses of a man's memory no longer blotted out with images of horrible death.

But note that in returning to Ruth, Adam has returned to Germany, or as close as he can get to it. Germany is home, more so than desert Israel with its Institute for Rehabilitation and Therapy. Perhaps, after all, home resides in the very place whose horrors we try to escape. And we may continue to nourish those horrors, fearing their disappearance. We may sojourn in a land that seems to promise something better, only to discover that we cannot leave that which formed us even though it nearly destroyed us. For Adam, Germany is home and not Israel. Klein is his god and not Jehovah. Adam will re-create his Germany in Israel. The question is: what kind of home will he create? In Israel, the promised land of the Jews, the answer to this question is still in agonizing doubt.

THE TRIUMPH OF DEATH (*HIS DAUGHTER*)

Adam Resurrected is the backstory for the people and events in *His Daughter*. Joseph Krieger, the novel's Israeli brigadier general, inhabits a world peopled by Adam Stein's contemporaries. He married a woman who shares some of Adam's profound madness. Joseph Krieger is not redeemed, however, while ultimately Adam is. It is sadly ironic that Joseph and his daughter literally do not survive, though both have been born in the "promised land" and are part of its history. Adam does survive, though he came from devastation. The two books are woven together by the thread of the Holocaust running throughout each of them, reflections on how the Nazi extermination continues far beyond its original murders.

His Daughter brings the Holocaust forward into the lives of Joseph Krieger, a fifty-year-old retired Army Brigadier General and his twenty-six-year old daughter Miriam, also an army officer. They live together in Tel Aviv, in the apartment where Joseph grew up and to which he returned shortly after his marriage to Miriam's mother Nina. Mother Nina, who has long ago left the family, arrived in Israel as a German refugee who survived one of the death camps. Father is housekeeper and cook for his grown child, asking only that she return home on time or notify him if she will be late. He asks nothing further of her, and is proud of his commitment to allowing his daughter maximum autonomy.

On the January day we meet father and daughter, Miriam does not return home at the appointed time nor does she call to report her whereabouts. The rest of the novel describes Joseph's search for his missing daughter, introduces us to the family and friends who fill his life and that of Miriam, acquaints us with Joseph's early years and the dissolution of his marriage along with his forced early retirement from the Israeli Army, and conjures up Miriam's liaisons, real and imagined. The book ends with Miriam's dead body finally discovered (she has been randomly murdered) and her father in a hospital bed neither dead nor alive after trying to kill himself with his ever-present army service revolver.

Miriam's disappearance begins the unraveling of the stories that give Joseph's life meaning, the crumbling of an old order replaced with desolation. Kaniuk (1988) invites us to look upon the contemporary emptiness of many of the early Israeli ideals that motivated Joseph, values inculcated in him as a young man. Gazing at Joseph, we question what makes an Israeli hero. Joseph's life is based entirely on what he learned to believe was essential to the survival of the State. At the center of those beliefs is a continuous admonition to bear in mind the enormity of the Holocaust. With his daughter gone and his beliefs proving to be futile, Joseph is a hollow man. Over and over, he asks himself how he could have been so ignorant of what was important in her life, so unaware of his daughter's wellsprings. In questioning his blindness to his daughter's realities, he begins to strip away his own closely held illusions.

Joseph represents the vaunted Israeli army warrior. He is a brigadier general, a career soldier, someone for whom the army is his life. He believes totally in Zionism and its tenets, telling us he couldn't have fought as bravely as he did in the Yom Kippur War (Israel's triumphalist defeat of the Egyptians in 1973) "if it hadn't been for what they had told me . . . I believed that I was truly alone, the privileged remnant of two thousand years of history. Even at primary school we taught ourselves how to fight" (89).

Joseph comes to see his life as barren of meaning as he realizes he's been oblivious to his daughter's abiding passion which gradually reveals itself. Basically she's been living a parallel existence to that required by her position as an army officer. Her life has primarily consisted of an ongoing relationship with Isaac Raphaeli, an Israeli soldier killed while serving under her father's command. Isaac's early death has driven her to find solace by consulting with a variety of people whose perspectives come to determine her activities. To Joseph, Miriam was occupied solely with fulfilling her military duties. His torment at her disappearance is made increasingly unbearable as he begins to understand that he had absolutely no idea of who she was, what she cared about, why she behaved as she did. He did not know what stories sustained her.

Deep in his soul Joseph suspects that Miriam arranged her disappearance as a way of shocking him into intense pain. In this, he is correct. For Miriam, her father's stolid response to life and his repression of feeling and doubt became a torment. Attempting to force him into experiencing some of her murky discomfort, she succeeds. She writes: "Daddy, I realized we were cursed. You were my cancer; I was yours. . . . You are what I'm trying to escape from" (171-73). Escape means death in her case and the destruction of his soul in her father's.

Miriam is an Israeli who has lost faith in the old stories, forfeiting her life before she can find new narratives that make more sense. Joseph's loss of his foundational stories is a result of the devastating loss of his daughter, she who was to have carried on the narrative for which he lived. Essential to that narrative was the admonition to fight at a moment's notice, to confront any present-day enemy who might plunge Israel into an existential threat. For Miriam, her father's embodiment of the past and its Zionist ideals was a life-threatening trap.

Alongside army general Joseph, we get portraits of two of his childhood friends. These men are also embodiments of the Zionist hero, their lives shaped by the inculcation of the need to be ever vigilant. Reuben has become highly successful in government with a key post in Foreign Intelligence. Joseph's other childhood friend, referred to only by his military title, has risen to the rank of chief of staff. Speaking of his comrades, Joseph speaks of the expectations they grew up with and continue to act on: "We knew that it was up to us, the new generation, to make the critical difference on the battlefield. The military option was our nation's only way to survive" (90).

Fighting, defending, keeping danger at bay is the *raison d'etre* for all of their actions. Joseph articulates the frameworks that defined them, remarking that "Solidarity was everything, forced as we were into the valley of death relying on fanatic courage, incited by team spirit, individual daring and the smell of the enemy around us" (94). Their bonding began early, and Joseph says that even as kids "we romanticized war and were always fighting against or hurting each other" (89). Continual battle in the service of Israel's survival is the only possible course of action. For Joseph and his friends, waging war is a constant. Belief in the military option as the primary guarantor of national survival lives on.

This triangle of men, friends from boyhood, is a set of recognizable figures in the Israeli defense hierarchy—brave army officer; intelligence bigwig and chief of staff. Starting out together as young, idealistic boys eager to fight for their new country, they believed what they were told about their manifest destiny. Over time, each of them moved in different yet successful directions. Now, however, they see themselves as middle-aged men being pushed aside by the next generation.

During a night of drinking and reminiscing, Joseph muses on the shifting realities that imperil the beliefs he once held so close and now mock the dreams he once had. Not only are the old ideals fading; the younger generation doesn't have the edge that made Joseph's life meaningful. He muses: "We were no longer the miniatures of the heroes we had wanted to be. . . . We were a transitional generation . . . but we still had to keep our eye on the younger generation who were forcing their way up . . . devoid of that dark feeling of the gunslinger at the edge of doom" (190-91).

Articulating the loss of power of early Zionists, Joseph expresses a fear of their displacement by a new generation unfamiliar with early guiding stories. In their transitional status, nothing remains clear-cut for Joseph and his comrades. He and his friends have lost the ideals that motivated them as younger men, and their sense of futility is not assuaged by the sense that they have created something worth giving their lives to. In addition, the fact that the coming generation may be less aware of present dangers is cause for alarm.

Their belief in sacrificing all for country—in fighting whomever and by any means necessary—is based on the stories they have been told all their lives. The destruction of the Jews in the Holocaust is one element of that story, but it is less compelling for Joseph the father than it is for Miriam, his daughter. Miriam is part of the new generation, a child of Israel. Born in Israel to a German mother as well as a native Israeli father, she is part of the Land itself. But she cannot live freely, given her legacy. Ultimately, she does not live at all. Miriam embodies the legacy of destruction continuing from generation to generation, no matter how she and her father attempt to forge something beyond the basic tenets of their existence.

To understand Miriam, it is essential to factor in her mother as much as her father. As a refugee from Nazi Germany, Nina carries unhealed wounds. Joseph tells us that his ex-wife "had escaped from a concentration camp where she'd slept in a dog kennel" (93). He goes on to describe her as a complicated mixture of resilience and anger, "enchanting harshness and . . . delicate femininity . . . she was a capricious woman and a sturdy rock, at once a sovereign princess and a hypochondriac . . . a lioness poised but poisoned" (92-93). Nina is a complex, deeply unhappy person. She is difficult to like, the volatility and harshness of her character keeping sympathy at bay. Her experiences in the death camps have irrevocably shaped a bitter response to life.

In the persons of Nina, Miriam's mother, and Joseph, her father, reside the seeds of the girl's destruction. Over and over again, Kaniuk makes the point that this coming together of disparate worlds built on a legacy of death cannot lead to anything positive. Miriam, his (Joseph's) daughter—his Israel—was born from the coupling between those who experienced the Holocaust and those who swore to avenge it. Miriam was born to parents who represent the destruction inherent in each of these worlds.

Kaniuk links Miriam's desperation to that of Israel itself. "His daughter," the book's title and a recurrent phrase throughout the narrative, refers both to Miriam and to the country itself. For Joseph, Israel the nation is as much his child as is his biological one. And the nation, like its child, is poisoned by the Holocaust. Commenting on Miriam's Israelness, the German side of the family is scornful. During Nina's pregnancy, her aunt tells Joseph: "Your food has poisoned her, your nation has poisoned her, everything here has poisoned her" (103). Nina wants no part of her child, and when Joseph tells her she has a daughter, she replies, "Don't get me mixed up with your bastard Miriam. I had nothing to do with it" (105). But whether as the daughter of Israel or a child of Germany, Miriam is certainly the offspring of something destructive, not life- giving. The tension between these Israeli and German elements plays out continually. Israeli Joseph cannot expunge the miseries of his Holocaust survivor wife. Nina cannot relinquish a past whose scars will never heal. Their daughter cannot reconcile these strains. In a letter to her father, Miriam herself sums up the impossible contradictions that make up both her personal legacy and the fate of Israel:

> In a marriage between an Israeli and a holocaust [sic] survivor, the holocaust survivor dominates. The Israeli is dwarfed; his life-giving Israeli seas recede. . . . After all, his parents' parents had lived and wailed in cellars. . . . The native Israeli . . . married to a holocaust survivor, lives with the secret of his wife's sadness, which infuses him like a poison. (50)

Joseph's German neighbor, the elderly survivor Madame Frau, underscores the impossibility of a happy outcome between Israeli and death camp survivor when she tells Joseph: "You don't grasp the nightmares we brought here with us. Miriam is grafted on two trees. One branch is old and rotten, but beautiful; the other is young and healthy, but ugly, utterly unappealing . . . all you really know is battles and bullets" (117). This is one terrible truth at the heart of the Zionist enterprise: trying to erect something that will banish the detritus of the past won't work. Battles and bullets create a new ugliness.

Joseph does not truly comprehend the Holocaust, and this is a supreme and telling irony. He was born in Israel, and the Germany of the Holocaust is a place he understands little. In a powerful set of contradictory images between the "light" Israel and the "dark" Germany, he says

> [Nina's] love was full of dark corners and desires which she had brought with her from places I couldn't recognize. . . . I was born by the sea in a luminous town full of balconies, sour cream and bananas, water-melon, ice-cream and falafel, lacking any profound investigation into mysteries or the secrets of forests, Nazi soldiers and two thousand years of Jewish history constituting the longest volume of tears. (112)

But it is what Nina represents—the Holocaust with all its impact—that motivates Joseph; he is "sold on it." He says, " it gave me strength, turning me into what I once dreamed of becoming as a child, a Hebrew soldier, a Hebrew knight, all on account of Nina. Perhaps *only* on account of her" (112). Madame Frau is correct when she says he doesn't understand the nightmares brought by the refugees. Sadly, in fighting for those tormented by terrible dreams, he contributes to a new darkness. And though he does not comprehend Nina's terrible origins, he fights battles in the name of it. The Holocaust gives him meaning. It is part of his very foundation.

During the course of *His Daughter*, Joseph becomes disillusioned with what he believed in as a young Zionist, losing the basis of his identity as he discovers the hidden layers that made up his beloved daughter. He comes to believe that his existence and hers lead only to disaster. In her person, Miriam encapsulates irresolvable conflicts. This child of Israel/Germany is far different from the orderly, on-time, obedient army officer daughter whom we meet in the book's first few pages. Rather she is a tormented and tormenting human being. As the story unfolds, and others appear whose lives have been touched by Miriam, strangely dissonant facts emerge. It turns out that Miriam has been hanging out at the family home of Isaac, the young dead soldier. For Isaacs's parents, Miriam is beyond reproach, a saintly and loving young woman upon whom they rely to transmit news from their dead son. Miriam has positioned herself as a spirit guide, and Isaac's parents ask her to communicate the dead Isaac's opinion on everything from the latest inflationary spike to the current political situation. The dead boy's father tells Joseph,

"You had a magnificent daughter . . . conscientious, ethical, intelligent, beautiful; . . . why did she have to fall in love with a dead boy?" (227).

But Noam, Isaac's deeply unhappy brother, sees a different Miriam. He tells Joseph, "Your daughter, after all, is deranged, a genuine lunatic. Certifiably so. Not some neurotic, surrounded by the romanticism of madness. . . . Your daughter is really nuts—she seems sane, talks to the point, always orderly with a charming smile, full of affection . . . but a psychotic from head to toe" (247). Speaking of their daughter to Joseph, Nina says, "She was the most dangerously self-destructive child I've ever met in my life. . . . She sat on the sidelines, waiting for herself like a cruel evil hunter out to kill rather than capture and in the end she snared herself" (212).

These latter portraits are of a young woman full of destructive impulses, willful and deranged. Within her fissured psyche are irreconcilable opposing traits. Miriam, this daughter of two Israelis, is a liar, a manipulator, a schemer. Israel, Joseph's symbolic and equally beloved daughter, is itself in a parlous condition. Miriam is preoccupied with loss and endless destruction, in love with death. Joseph says, "those sad eyes of hers . . . had somehow trapped two thousand years of grief . . . that ancient gloom, which came with her territory, separated her from the rest of the world and declared her irrevocable terror at the prospect of a new day" (2). Her last letter to Joseph tells him "Death is constant. . . . Death never loses. . . . Death and my addiction to it released me from the fear I was hooked on. . . . Alongside death I no longer had the sensation of dread" (277). Miriam takes comfort in the certainty of death, coming to prefer it to the slow poisoning of daily dreads.

His Daughter is a novel about pervasive ongoing trauma in the land of Israel. Joseph, Miriam, and Nina are all haunted by a sense that whatever they do is overshadowed by doom. For Nina, the stench of the concentration camps cannot and will not fade. For Miriam, her father's military actions have resulted in fatalities in general and one in particular which she cannot expunge. Joseph's life as a soldier in the service of Zionism is now a nihilistic existence: "all I felt was that when I placed my hand to my body smack to where my pistol would be, I would hear my daughter speak . . . she and Nina sat in some murky spot inside me, demanding that canteen of blood with which I had commenced my real existence" (233).

Through his characters, Kaniuk illuminates elements that perpetuate cycles of violence and wasted lives within a land that promised the possibility of renewal in an escape from ancient ills. Joseph is the Jewish hero-soldier-warrior so valued by those who insist that Jews will never again be defeated by enemies stronger than themselves. He is the apotheosis of the New Jew, fearless in battle, calm under pressure, loyal to the land of Israel, unquestioning in his willingness to make whatever sacrifices are necessary to defend the land, never pausing to consider what the personal costs might be. In the end—actually, long before the end—he has sacrificed his wife, his daughter, and his own life.

Kaniuk invites us to witness a web of disillusion and destruction, the unquestioned narratives of Zionism and the centrality of the Holocaust poisoning those who see founding stories as immutable. Miriam functions as a spirit guide who navigates the space between Isaac's living parents and their dead son. Channeling the dead Isaac is the chief way in which she communicates on a meaningful level. It is not to her father that she speaks regularly, nor to her mother or her friends. As she tells her father, she awakens daily to "another day's death" (4). Death surrounds her, in the legacy of her Holocaust mother, the military exploits of her swashbuckling father, her own work as an army officer. Her primary companion, the person to whom she feels closest, is a dead man. The novel insists on the presence of an all-perverse sense that what was to have given life and hope—the birth and maintenance of Israel—has resulted in a morbid sense of impasse.

As her father is the "New Jew," Miriam is the "New Israeli" formed by elements of a profoundly distressed past and a seriously compromised present. Miriam was given birth by people representing two major markers of contemporary Jewish life: the Holocaust survivor and the Israeli Army officer. Embodying such poles, this body cannot transcend all the death surrounding it. If we read *His Daughter* as an allegory of contemporary Israel, Joseph the father and Nina the mother beget Miriam the daughter who is witness to and product of an alliance in a land of continuously ruptured endings. In another letter to her father, Nina writes, "I'm still your daughter, two sides to one catastrophe. . . . What a book of lamentations I've ended up with" (169-70).

Speaking to his ex-wife Nina about their daughter, Joseph says, "At one time, in Morocco, young Jewish brides whose betrotheds had died, would marry them in the cemetery making them husband and wife on both sides of death. . . . Did Miriam marry death?" (204). The answer is surely "yes, she did." Her story is a litany of sorrows. We may wonder where the new bridegrooms are to be found if all the Miriams are not to die barren and her Israels are not to perish as well.

NOTE

1. See March of the Living (http://motl.org/)

Chapter Two

Chaos and Jerusalem's Discontents

Orly Castel-Bloom

If I forget thee, O Jerusalem, let my right hand forget her cunning . . . If I do not remember thee, let my tongue cleave to the roof of my mouth . . . Happy shall he be, that taketh and dasheth thy little ones against the stones. (Psalm 137)

For Israel-centric true believers, Israel can do no wrong. It is the Holy Land, birthplace of the biblical patriarchs Abraham, Isaac, and Jacob. The lives of Noah, Moses, and King David are certified by the Hebrew Bible. The biblical document serves as the prooftext for present-day claims that Israel belongs to the Jewish people, regardless of who else lived there in modern times. Zionists on the political right as well as those closer to the center often insist that Israel belongs to the Jews because it was this very place to which God sent Abraham, telling him in Genesis 13:15 "I give all the land that you see to you and to your offspring forever."[1] Regarding allegiance to Israel as a cornerstone of Jewish identity, Israelcentric Jews view the country as their true homeland whether or not they have been there or ever intend to go.

Neither Gaza nor the West Bank exists; these territories are the historical Jewish Judea and Samaria. As they were in ancient times, so are they now: property given to the Jews by God. The burgeoning fundamentalist settler movement draws militant strength from its belief in God-given certainty, joined in this certitude by some fundamentalist Christian Zionists who lend moral support and hard currency to the dream of a land free of nonresident aliens like Palestinians. In the Christian Bible, the birth and death of Jesus Christ are said to have occurred in this sacred space. Fundamentalist Christians doggedly support a present-day Israeli stance that insists on tightly

21

monitored borders and little or no willingness to trade land for peace. For these Christians, the land belongs to the Jews now and in future will be the site of the Second Coming of Christ. Their voices, and their dollars, help keep present-day policies in place.[2]

For it is not only Israelcentric Jews who view this country as a designated Holy Land with special status and legitimacy grounded in ancient texts. In the eyes of many Christians, Israel is fundamental to the return of the Messianic Age, the staging ground for their own redemption. All three so-called Abrahamic religions—Judaism, Christianity, and Islam—focus on Israel in general and Jerusalem in particular as an originary source of their revered religious narratives. From the Jordan River to Mt. Sinai, Bethlehem to the Dead Sea, Israel is densely layered with sacred places as described in the Hebrew Bible, the Koran, and the New Testament. The Abrahamic religions' framing narratives, the master myths of their believers, take place in Israel. The country's artifacts and memories cement ties that bind over centuries and over countries. Religionists insist that because it is holy, Israel is subject to a different set of laws than those governing less-exalted nations. Claims and counterclaims as to who is entitled to what portion of this beleaguered land base key arguments on their own particular reading of biblical text.

Furthermore, the special bond between the United States and Israel draws much of its strength from a shared notion of national exceptionalism. Blessed by a benevolent god, both the United States. and Israel see themselves as fulfilling a manifest destiny that sets them apart from less enlightened nations. Yes, some United States-Israel closeness stems from concerns around national security, and an agreed-upon Western definition of democracy. But the bottom line for both of these nations is found in the much invoked notion of a shared Judeo-Christian heritage. These two nations partially understand one another because each believes they inhabit a divinely ordained space. When you believe the claim to your country comes from the desires of a god who has picked you out from among the multitudes, it's hard to do business with people who don't buy into that notion. Huddling together against challenges to their hegemony, Israel and the United States support some of each other's darkest claims to nonaccountability.

Raising the emotional stakes is the city of Jerusalem, which holds pride of place in Abrahamic religions' claims to sacred space. For Jews, it is their most holy city. Joining them in revering it are Christians, for whom Christ's tomb is located in Jerusalem's Church of the Holy Sepulcre, and Muslims, who believe the prophet Mohammed ascended to heaven from Jerusalem's Dome of the Rock. Alas, this exact spot is where many Jews believe the Second Temple stood. Its destruction in 70 ce has not ended the longing by fundamentalist Jews to rebuild the ancient temple at the very same location. It is impossible to overstate the centrality of Jerusalem's mythic power. The divine, as variously conceived by the followers of three religions, holds a huge stake in the local real estate. It's a heavy weight for a twenty-first-century city to bear, a difficult burden to mute all the angry insistent voices clamoring for control of this sacred symbol.

It is surely ironic that the majority of Israel's founding generation was secular; these were persons for whom the beliefs and practices of religious Jews were not to be taken seriously. There is evidence that early Zionist leaders like Theodore Hertzl and David Ben Gurion cynically used religion only to undergird their claims to legitimacy when Israel was first established.[3] They had no desire to promote religious Judaism in any form. Little could they predict that in contemporary Israel, fundamentalist Judaism would be deeply entrenched and disastrously linked to nationalist aspirations.

Fundamentalists, particularly in the settlements, wield disproportionate power in setting national policy and their growing numbers have established stubbornly rooted "facts on the ground."[4] A vocal and powerful segment in the U.S. persists in the notion that this land is beyond reproach, literally sacred, and must be defended at all costs. The Christian right in America forms partnerships with unquestioning defenders of this putative holy land's policies and actions. A worldwide series of alliances bases its beliefs on the idea that Israel, this small speck of land, is at the center of a God-determined universe. What's occurring in present-day Israel has ramifications far beyond its still-contested borders. The conflict seems unresolvable much of the time, repeating endless cycles of terror, violence, retribution. If one element of insanity is to persist in acts that repeatedly lead to mayhem, destruction, and death, the situation in Israel-Palestine surely qualifies it as a crazy place.

LAUGHTER AMIDST THE RUINS (*DOLLY CITY*)

Enter Orly Castel-Bloom, a fifty-two-year-old writer and resident of Tel Aviv. Her Israeli characters in *Dolly City* are unhinged, exhibiting behaviors both irrational and destructive. Savage in her satirical wit, she critiques a country she sees as increasingly reckless and that responds to current dilemmas in fundamentally dysfunctional ways. In her fictive world, people spin out of control and events take on a surreal caste. Castel-Bloom's attacks spare no one, mowing down such targets as clueless politicians, perverse medical doctors run amuck in a candy store of available chemicals, overdeveloped towns and cities where everyone is in a rush to nowhere, idiotic television presenters, and sanctimonious social workers who atone for past sins by bullying the poor souls unfortunate enough to be under their care. She brilliantly satirizes every aspect of Israeli life, both institutional and individual, verbally eviscerating those people for whom counterclaims to any parts of this ancient land are unimaginable.

At the center of her pulverizing satire in this howlingly funny and bitter book, *Dolly City* is the state of the State of Israel. Living in the so-called holy land, Castel-Bloom does not buy into any exalted notions about this place in either myth or reality. On the contrary, she suggests that Israel is a crazily dysfunctional place peopled by out-of-control individuals who are near-savages in their behaviors and attitudes. The ferocious humor and bloodcurdling satire of her books challenges the notion that there is anything holy about Israel or anything sacred about its people and their lives. While all the authors in this study write of a land and a people that are deeply flawed, no one does it in the over-the-top, no-holds-barred manner of Castel-Bloom. Her relentless, discomfiting prose leaves no room for any notion that those who populate Israel have constructed a place worthy of emulation—or for that matter, a place worthy of being inhabited at all.

Castel-Bloom (1997) is not writing a realistic depiction of life in a land beset by solvable problems. Readers are not invited to contemplate the root causes of Israel's skewed responses nor to consider rational ways in which situations might be addressed. In her allegorical novel, we are confronted with an ersatz doctor, Dolly, who carves up her illegitimate son to see if he is all right: "I opened up his stomach and I held an organ parade" (37). Dolly is Mother Israel, a bitter swipe at Israel's predominantly male-centered narratives, whose relationship with Son (for so she has named her offspring) concretizes some of the country's most destructive tendencies. The place Dolly City is clearly a stand-in for Jerusalem, a city whose symbolic attractions continue to inspire near mythic acts of madness. Castel-Bloom's fantasy world rockets along, leaving us to contemplate profound disorder with no foreseeable way out of the morass. Dolly is a dysfunctional Everywoman representing a level of goofy madness that is truly monumental.

Interpreting *Dolly City* poses a challenge in conveying the essence of its satiric humor. It's like trying to explain why a joke is funny. The book's comedy is never benign. It's a morbid humor coming out of despair, a realization of how impossibly messed-up everything is. Meaningless absurdity can lead to anguished tears or to bemusement tinged with deep pain. Orly Castel-Bloom's human comedy stems from a sense of futility, recognition of a state of affairs which can only be met with lunatic laughter. Neither for her, nor for her character Dolly, is there room to lament. In their fundamentally hopeless situations, with no foreseeable way forward, the sanest response is to exaggerate people and situations by highlighting the implacable madness of their circumstances.

Castel-Bloom's style and mordant wit place her squarely in a line of satirists like Jonathan Swift, and there are intriguing parallels between Swift's eighteenth-century Ireland and Castel-Bloom's twenty-first-century Israel. Swift brilliantly mocked British cruelty to the Irish, suggesting in *A Modest Proposal* that Irish babies are a most delicious foodstuff. Properly prepared and cooked, they make a savory meal for the discerning palate. Among other acts, Dolly sews her son to her back so she can worry less about being separated from him. While no doubt this is better than cooking and eating him, the idea is the same. Both authors exaggerate phenomena based on actual situations, mocking what is absurd in the real world to let in the healing force of humor.

Reading Castel-Bloom in a line going back to fellow satirist Swift gives a much needed sense of perspective for the reader who may take some comfort that Swift's Ireland was riven in ways not unlike present-day Israel. Both Castel-Bloom's Israel and Swift's Ireland are in a parlous state. In Swift's Ireland, the potato famine threatened to wipe out whole villages. Contemporary Israel is in a continual state of military alert, its government insisting it must remain battle-ready to combat the ever-looming possibility of terrorist attacks.

Eighteenth-century Ireland and twenty-first-century Israel both had a profoundly important relationship with the British Empire. Swift's Ireland was part of Britain and did not become a separate country until after World War I. Israel became a modern nation only after World II when the British left yet another mess, partitioning the so-called holy land and giving part of it to the Zionists. Influenced by their binding relationship to a greater imperial power, both countries wrestle with transitions that arise from separating into nation-states with their own identities.

Castel-Bloom's work, like Swift's, unambiguously resists, challenges, and mocks the national identity Israel seeks to promote in its own interest, an Israel formatively modeled on the hegemonic Eurocentric West. The strength of the novel lies in piling on one small detail after another to illuminate Dolly's mad schemes and justify her bizarre actions. Insane ideas are given a patina of rationality. Over-the-top hilarious suggestions as to how seemingly intractable problems might be addressed are presented with deadpan certitude. Of course it's no solution to Ireland's poverty and overpopulation to sell babies so they may be eaten for dinner. Of course it's not rational to cut up a child and monitor his health by examining innards in an organ check, as Dolly continually does. Of course it's not a great idea to carve up a tiny piece of Middle Eastern land and assail its inhabitants by repeated assaults justified by inventive and often dubious premises.

Swift's *A Modest Proposal* is still shockingly funny though it was written over two hundred and seventy-five years ago. Whether Castel-Bloom, like Swift, will stand the test of time is less important than the fact that her writing today examines Israel's foibles with a penetrating honesty cloaked in satiric excess. Forget rapier wit—a blunt-edged sword lays waste to folly of all kinds in this startling and sadly all too imaginable satiric landscape.

It is of course possible to read *Dolly City* "straight," to see it as a sad vision of a dystopian world hovering on the brink of extinction. But that is to miss out on the sheer joy of reveling in Castel-Bloom's inventiveness. The book is a comic masterpiece. The best advice is to read it and laugh bitterly, for the novel gets at agonizing truths about a time and a place that are, indeed, teetering on the edge.

We first meet our narrator Dolly at the age of thirty and take our leave of her nineteen years later. The story concludes with forty-nine-year-old Dolly being prematurely put away by Son in a shelter for the aged, with a glimpse of her reading about his improbable escapades in a newspaper borrowed from a fellow inmate. This assumes, of course, that we can believe anything Dolly tells us. Dolly is deranged, and we may question anything and everything that comes from her telling. She is surely the quintessential unreliable narrator. While her narration of the book's events is dominated by nutty, distorted views, Dolly's thoughts and actions are basically plausible once the reader makes a willing suspension of disbelief in the interest of inhabiting this topsy-turvy world.

The dominant paradigm for everything that occurs in the novel is located in the relationship between Dolly and Son, and in their allegorical representations of aspects of Israel. Dolly dominates throughout, and Son exists mainly as an extension of her crazy self. Sometimes that extension is literal as when Dolly sews him to her own body. Their Mother/Son enmeshment mirrors an attachment by Israeli citizens to a powerful country led about by fanciful policy makers. Dolly is the zany Israeli government ineptly parenting an uneasy population of sons and daughters, while Son personifies the hapless citizen upon whom the State acts out ever-more destructive fantasies. Bullying Mother Israel leads her citizens down a reckless path. Castel-Bloom shines a blinding light on the road being taken.

Dolly insists that her body is the authority which will protect Son from any marauder, be it from a person or a pathogen, and the price for this protection must be paid. Gazing at her sleeping son after she has performed yet another act of invasive surgery on him, Dolly remarks, "There was an unspoken agreement between us that he deserved it" (37). A subliminal pact dictates the terms of what happens between crazy mother and the child whose life she directs—as there is tacit agreement between citizens and government to permit the status quo in a country that encourages waking moments filled with fear. Dolly's body can never promise impregnable safety, nor can the Israeli body politic find safety in the government's attempts to keep its citizens safe from harm by primarily military means.

Castel-Bloom signals the efficacy of an allegorical reading by her use of capital letters to personify abstract ideas. The allegorical hints begin with Dolly's naming of the infant she finds in a plastic garbage bag lying on the roadside. Calling him Son "so that if anyone ever called him son-of-a-bitch he could beat them up for both of us" (20) suggests a figure who transcends the ordinary definition of offspring. The capital S refers not just to a proper name but to an allegorical being more significant than simply an individual male child. The novel is a tale of the mad journey of Dolly and Son—of Mother Israel and her sons—as they blunder their way into outlandish situations in a phantasmagoric world. Implicit in their insane itinerary is the notion that they inhabit a place and a time where the ordinary rules of reality have been suspended. Of course it's an everyday fact of life that "Kurdish refuges . . . take over [Dolly's] apartment . . . sitting in the Jacuzzi and using [her] shampoo," (78) and it's no big deal that in Dolly's streetside Instant-Relief-from-Pain stall, she injects people with Pepsi Cola when sedatives aren't available. Dolly City is one big, crazy funhouse.

Suspending rational expectations and replacing them with unreal scenarios underscores the ever-present fact that Dolly's world doesn't play by any recognizable rules. Thus does Castel-Bloom's satirical allegory challenge the idea of Israel as a place where everyday norms may be pushed aside in the interest of a perceived higher reality based on such things as a literal reading of scripture. A holy land is not to be judged like other contemporary nation-states. Confronted with the symbolism of this place, how is a person to describe its real-life flaws and all-too-human errors in judgment? Orly Castel-Bloom offers a reality check by savaging conventionally held notions of the nature of this beleagured country.

As narrator and main character Dolly is allegorical Mother Israel, so Dolly City is a stand-in for Jerusalem itself. Once again, capital letters alert us to a place emblematic of something far beyond an ordinary place name. Looking at a map of this metropolis, Dolly sees "the Wells of Despair, the Lakes of Fear, the Swamps of Boredom" (139). Ordinary wells are not temporarily dysfunctional sources of water but containers of dashed dreams. Lakes hold disquieting fear, and swamps an overwhelming sense of ennui. It's a damning list of negative attributes. The personification of painful geography is further evidence that Jerusalem, a.k.a. Dolly City, is a negative, life-denying place.

For Dolly, it's a dreadful place, a fragmented, whorish city which freaks her out and adds to already strong feelings of overwhelming restless frenzy. She insists that, "Dolly City is driving me crazy" (57). Like Jerusalem, Dolly City is at the center of a small and locked-in universe; it's the chaotic center of a troubled world. Dolly experiences it as an enveloping, deeply unhappy, destructive place: "The most demented city in the world," and "one big grave" where "everyone is tormented, and everyone tries in vain to escape" (88, 100).

A character who is leaving it forever says that "[Dolly City is] not a place. It's an ugly, disgusting, stinking, filthy, boring, depressing town" (100). Dolly even goes so far as to say "I'd like to ask: given that Dolly City is such a terrible place why don't the Americans bomb it? . . . Why don't a few enlightened nations get together and blast this city right off the map?" (110).

For her, Dolly City is a junked-up place full of psychic wreckage. It cannot be redeemed, and would be better destroyed. Castel-Bloom's savage wit eviscerates any notion of Jerusalem as a golden city of hope and religious idealism. For Dolly, it's basically uninhabitable.

Terrible as Dolly City is, however, it remains home, a place to which Dolly is profoundly attached and from which she never ventures forth. "The fog of Dolly City—it envelopes you like a silk gown, pricks you like an acupuncture, goes straight to your nervous system" (117). Trying to imagine life outside its walls is impossible. Dolly cannot do it: "There were rare moments when I would try with all my might and main to feel part of a world far wider than Dolly City, but is was almost impossible. I was my own prisoner—I couldn't escape" (45). Inextricably bound to the city, any possibility of moving away is unthinkable.

So it is with many of the current residents of the "real" Dolly City— Jerusalem. As bad as things are, its residents are bound to this place and will go to any lengths to keep it as it has always been for them. Any attempt to reconfigure the city to make it more equally accessible and more open to competing religious claims is met with militant resistance. Jerusalem's Old City is divided into Jewish, Christian, Armenian, and Arab quarters. They are separate and unequal and likely to remain so. The raucous, fractionated city keeps its hold on the religious imagination of the Abrahamic religions, and these three monotheisms keep a tight grip on buildings and neighborhoods which they see as pieces of their holy turf. Increasingly, fundamentalist settlers buy land and establish facts on the ground in the interest of making Jerusalem the undivided capital of the Jewish state.

Attempts to make Jerusalem an international city owned by no single entity have proved futile, with mention of it falling under United Nations mandate met with derision and blocked at every turn. Any thought of allowing Palestinians to set up their capital in East Jerusalem, a place to which they are linked through their history, is unthinkable to the official Israel and its U.S. backers.[5] Jerusalem remains fragmented, noisy, dysfunctional, ugly in its bitter divisions and enraged inhabitants.

As she longs in vain to free herself from its tentacles, a place she detests, Dolly damns it as "a city without a base, without a past, without an infrastructure. The most demented city in the world" (88). These are heretical notions for the millions of religionists for whom Jerusalem is sacrosanct. Saying it has no past is an outrageously blasphemous statement, followed closely by accusing it of being the world's most demented place. Harsh indictments by our mad narrator paint a troubled metropolis with little saving grace.

Her rhetoric leads us to consider how mad our allegorical Dolly is. Quite mad, as it turns out. She is a person of gigantic excess, monumental indiscretion, feverish temperament, uncontrollable impulses, and murderous responsiveness. We encounter an outlandish creature representing extreme possibilities, embodying everything that has gone amiss in Israel. In her aggressiveness, delusions, beat-up psyche, and cancerous soul, Dolly has gone past all limits and broken all restraining boundaries. Furthermore, her madness is fed by the realities of the place in which she resides. In short, Dolly is deranged in large part because her country has gone off the rails. Dolly's madness is tied to the disorder in the fabric of her country.

Madness is a predator which feasts on the soul and takes over the human mind, she tells us. Dolly compares this conquering of the mind with the conquering of territories like Judea, Samaria, and Gaza: "And if a state like the State of Israel can't control the Arabs in the territories how can anybody expect me, a private individual, to control the occupied territory inside me?" (110). This could hardly be more explicit. Dolly's psyche has been invaded, inhabited by madness and its discontents. She has an enemy living inside her, and it is subordinating everything. Unable to cast out the chaos, she is constantly in thrall to it. As her nation is out of balance in its role of occupier of the land of others, so is her mind unable to subdue its invasion by chaos. In fact, she thinks "the state should pay for the psychiatric treatment of its citizens since the state was unbalancing their minds" (141).

Occasionally, Dolly comments on herself with astonishing lucidity in moments of clarity that temporarily lift her out of self-destructiveness. Her perceptions connect the dots with stunning accuracy. While insisting on the one hand that she is as trapped as her country, another part of her revels in her lunacy. She boasts that "crazy people like to say that being crazy is stronger than they are. Not me—I may be crazy but being crazy is not stronger than I am" (120). It's clear that Dolly has no desire to move beyond madness; rather, she seeks to redefine it. In her view, she is actually in control of her aberrance. She is strong enough to coexist with—and even master—her insanity. This suggests that craziness is an integral part of her repertoire, valuable and not to be discarded.

In short, it works well to be mad. Why cast out something that functions so effectively? Why indeed if that very nonrationality permits you to exclude from view the disintegration taking place right in front of your eyes? The trick is to insist that however cockeyed your worldview, distortion is desirable and to be trusted as a more reliable filter for truth. Living with madness, in fact, is to be preferred over sanity, which is the real danger that must be held at bay. Any sign of well-being is fraught with too much danger, a possible mortal threat. Dolly remarks of her absent son, "his letters showed more than a spark of sanity. The boy was happy . . . [but] you had to watch out for it . . . he [might] suddenly die of cancer, just like that. . . . whenever I detected a note of happiness in my son's letters, my heart filled with anxiety" (170–71).

It's better to be on the edge—to live in a state of frenzied discomfort and hand-to-mouth improvised survival—than to dream that things can right themselves. Happiness is to be feared as an emotion that evokes anxiety and anticipation of loss. If Son experiences joy, Dolly will lose him. It follows that she must do everything in her power to keep this destructive joy at bay. So must Israel keep harmony somewhere away over an ever-receding horizon. A shift towards rapprochement might destroy the States' uneasy equilibrium. There is comfort to be had from the certainty of an ever-present enemy. Dolly watches for any sign that might indicate that Son is changing, and she will quash his burgeoning moves towards another state of mind.

Dolly occasionally recognizes the soul-destroying quality of her wildly skewed perspective, for instance when she remarks: "Already I was resigned to living with this cancer I had in my soul (yes, you could certainly say that I was suffering from cancer of the soul)" (170). But she can live with a bombed-out soul; she cannot live with that elusive and scary thing called Hope. Furthermore, she fears that ridding herself of madness will destroy her. So bound up is her identity with being crazy that letting go of madness provokes a fear of death. We humans define ourselves through a series of traits, however destructive, and so is it with nations. Citizens and governments buy into national myths, holding tightly to beliefs about what their country represents. Changing the story of a nation is no less difficult than shifting personal stories. Israel cannot simply move away from the stories it tells itself of being continually imperiled, no matter that its military might is world-renowned for its power. Nor can it easily reimagine its borders, for to do so would be to cast aside a framework which serves its interests well enough.[6] Israel's government grows ever more intransigent in its reluctance to trade any land for peace. And it is growing less likely for this nation's citizens to imagine that others have their own story which is equally compelling as a national myth.[7]

As Dolly says, the human race has not yet found "a way to kill madness without killing the madman, too" (111). For her, there is no way to destroy one without eliminating the other. Healing herself is an impossible task, and it is inconceivable that surcease from omnipresent madness is possible. Better to disregard chaos and let delusion in all its manifestations triumph. "I discovered the way to fight my insanity—ignore it. I taught myself to treat my madness in the same way you behave towards a madman you meet in the street—humor him and move on" (123). Humor the settler who insists on destroying Palestinian homes so his family can occupy them. Humor the government which refuses to talk to those it dismisses as illegitimate. Humor the policy makers who insist on military means as the only way to ensure security. Ignore alternatives.

While Dolly can overlook her internal crazy self, she cannot fully disregard that which surrounds and helps keep intact her "cancer of the soul." Her madness takes multiple forms, but concentrates itself primarily in distortions centered at the site of the physical body. Corporeal selves are mutilated, diseased, dysfunctional. Illness and death are everywhere, and Dolly cannot turn away from physical breakdown and decay. The body is where the madness she walks away from goes to wait for her. Cancer is a recurring metaphor, lying in wait to claim Dolly, Son, and everyone else. It is the ultimate malignant force, even for inanimate objects: "I saw cancerous growths . . . on the barrels of tar, on the wheels of the buses, on the electricity poles, on the trees, on the wheels of the cars, on the newspapers; wherever I looked, malignant, terminal, spreading tumors danced before my eyes . . . the metastases were taking over the world; it was their finest hour" (72–73).

Accepting her account of this mortally afflicted world and letting her bleary gaze guide us, we experience a place on the brink of disintegration. No one and nothing is safe, certainly not her beloved Son (if Dolly can be said to have a beloved anything). Again and again, we watch Dolly react with horror to the notion that cancer is lying around every corner, waiting to strike. She has told us that while Son was happy "he might suddenly die of cancer, just like that" (171). An ancient pediatric medical text that Dolly consults "described horrible children's diseases that were widespread and fatal at the time . . . [and she] couldn't help connecting these diseases with my son" (24–25). In order to ensure Son's survival and to protect him from harm, Dolly has him surgically sewn to her back.

Trying to keep Son safe involves multiple surgeries, countless attempts to inspect and replace vital organs, an unrelenting gaze quick to spot anything which no doubt signals his untimely end. Never is Son safe; never can she cease her eternal vigilance: "My concern for his health knew no bounds. . . . I would close up the place I had opened and open the place that was closed . . . Until it reached a stage where every inch of his body had been opened. It was an impossible life, but I lived it nonetheless" (66).

No matter that Dolly realizes her approach makes no sense and that the life she lives is untenable. She is helpless in the face of an addiction to destruction. Her sense of danger has become a medication, pulling her in with the excitement of possible calamity. Living with continual danger has become a drug, a craving for the energy that comes from hyper-viligance.

A fear of deadly contamination, like that prevailing in Dolly City, reenforces the idea that anyone outside of one's known universe is not only illegitimate but also extremely dangerous. One of the tools for maintaining the status quo is to use the power engendered by terror. A terrified population is often a passive population, willing to believe the worst about a perceived enemy. Recognizing that constant fear also enchants, politicians may create a kingdom ruled by it. As Dolly says, "I was terrified and my terror had a magic, addictive effect . . . it was quite exciting" (25). She reminds us that

fear can be an habitual intoxicant. It's worth the cost in lives lost and maimed
to experience the thrill of being scared.

Focusing on the body as a locus of death and disease is not an uncommon
trope for maladies of the soul. Bodily malfunctions in human beings reflect
gross dysfunctions in the country where Dolly lives. In Dolly City, the malo-
dorousness of people's bodies is a continuous reminder of the mess in which
the inhabitants of this city exist. Anything to do with the body is unhealthy,
distorted, an indication of surrounding decay. Under constant attack from
bodily harm, people avoid sexual contact lest it infect.

For Dolly, sex is a manic, distasteful act indulged in only by cretinous
individuals with little or no sense. There are frequent reminders of how
sexual attractions and activities contribute to her enveloping madness. Sex is
stupid and vulgar at best, deathly at worst. Even an innocent kiss from Son
holds the possibility of killing her. When Son, sewn to her back, hugs Dolly
she panics: "before I knew what hit me he would land a kiss on me, and a
kiss meant cancer of the teeth, the mouth, and the gums" (91). As always, the
reasoning is skewed, the example wildly exaggerated, and the conclusion
insane. But avoiding the kiss of death from Son, like so much in the novel, is
laughable in its weird inventiveness.

Hysteria is a constant for Dolly, a hyped-up response to a world full of
deranged people performing grotesque deeds. Dolly herself is, of course,
deranger-in-chief. Just after secreting herself in a vehicle, Dolly tells us
matter-of-factly that she kills the driver. This is the first of many casual
killings she enacts. The word "murder," while appropriate, is too strong and
misses the comic madness of the off-handed manner in which she disposes of
people interfering with whatever mad goal she is pursuing. Getting rid of
people who annoy her is a casual act of disposal, one done as easily as
hanging up on an annoying caller. Lives are not taken seriously in Dolly
City. Other people's bodies are hers for the taking, and killing is an act
without consequence. In her notebook, Dolly divides the page into columns:
"one for those I'd killed out of negligence, one for those I'd killed by mistake
and one for those I'd lammed into with everything I've got" (95). But the
notebook is left on a bench, an unimportant reminder of lives lost in crazy
Dolly City. Bodies are either sick, disposable, ugly, or disgusting; they are
worth no more than a passing and disposable notation.

Underneath Dolly's madness resides a great well of fear expressing itself
chiefly in a terror of annihilation by the ubiquitous cancer monster. The
disease ransacks everything, destroying with unabating ferocity. In the face
of this near-certain death, she must be constantly vigilant. The very country
itself is under attack by illness, in danger of being destroyed by ravaging
pathogens. As individual bodies break down and die, so too does society
dissolve under the onslaught of a relentless foe. The body politic is diseased,
the relentless onslaught of cancer a potent metaphor for a country which

experiences itself in a continual state of crisis. Along with Dolly describing cancer on the wheels, pole, and trees, Dolly also believes that "the valleys have got cancer, the fields . . . the mountains, the rocks—everything" (117).

As Dolly sees cancer everywhere, so does Israel see its own imminent destruction should it for a moment desist from eternal vigilance. The check-points, the military, the separation wall will keep out the cancers lurking in every corner. Like Dolly, the country will stop at nothing to save its beloved Sons. Though the cure may kill them, there can be no alternative. As Dolly says, "I, as a mother, had to fight against all these troubles; I had to protect this child against evil afflictions and natural disasters. I had to keep him safe" (25–6). She inoculates Son in one go with every injection she can find, remarking that "I couldn't stop myself; I couldn't control my maternal instinct" (26).

In this grotesquely comic exaggeration of demented mothering, Dolly sees herself as an embattled and isolated figure fighting against all comers to save and protect her child: "I declared war to the bitter end: Dolly against the rest of the world" (26). Excessive inoculations and multiple invasive surgeries to reveal Son's every organ are just the cost of keeping him well. It's insane, absurd, an inventive demonstration of the idea that to save a village, one must destroy it. Son is almost destroyed, turning blue and requiring emergency resuscitation. The child's near destruction comes, obviously, from the mother's self-confessed inability to control her instincts.

This statement, like everything Dolly says, is delivered without irony. The humor, of course, stems partially from errant nonsense being delivered with conviction in a tone of unwavering certainty. Throughout *Dolly City*: the most outrageous, unbelievable acts are described as though they make sense. Of course, Dolly will give the child inoculations that almost kill him. Not only is her child brought near death, but Dolly is so distressed that she herself comes close to death due to an overdose. She passes out, telling us that she is now clinically dead, only to be revived three hours later by her mother. We are reminded, however, that in the Herculean effort of making the world safe—for democracy, for the survival of the State, for whatever—it is not only the destruction of another we must fear, but destroying ourselves as well. Dolly will frequently come close to killing herself; she will continually go to absurd lengths to protect Son; she will lose her mind more than once. Yet she will never learn that exceeding boundaries and going over the edge tends to create little besides mayhem and wreckage. Dolly has created her own world with its own logic and its own rationales. Cutting herself off from a larger world reenforces the certainty that there are no truths aside from those created inside her own mind.

Fear is partially fed by the language used to invoke it, often by employing inappropriate language to describe actions. Once again Dolly is an instructive teacher. Words are abused and meanings turned inside out, as when references to the healing of Son actually describe acts of destruction. Ancient texts are cited to undergird lunatic responses to the present moment, as Dolly demonstrates a linguistic perversity in using centuries-old documents to cope with contemporary realities. As Dolly is diagnosing Son, she notes: "my eye was caught by a sixteenth-century book on pediatrics. . . . I began reading. It was written in Latin and described horrible children's diseases that were widespread and fatal at the time" (24).

Not only does Dolly rely on an out-of-date book on children's diseases, she uses another ancient book, the Bible, to identify two parts of her country as Judea and Samaria. Israel's settlers insist on this biblical nomenclature when talking about disputed lands which others see as part of the present-day West Bank. To name something is to own it, and calling the occupied territories Judea and Samaria is to take possession of them in the name of one's own text and one's own excluding vision. Dolly knows how to do that, twisting language to make the world confirm to her view of it. Inscribing a map based on a recollection of what the Bible says, as Dolly does, provides another pointed satiric reminder that many arguments as to what constitutes "Greater Israel" are based on references to so-called biblical truths. Using ancient texts as a guide to her mapmaking, she is at one with an Orthodox Israeli rabbi who remarked, "The state . . . was 'entirely sacred and without blemish. It is an exalted heavenly manifestation' of God's return to Zion." Gorenberg, 2006, (276).

It's not just textual language that Dolly turns inside out. Her actions express comic perversion as she does one thing while calling it something else. Her words exemplify cosmic lunacy, as when she flies to Germany, goes to an orphanage and "trie[s] all the kidneys of all forty babies in the home" (54) until she finds a new kidney for Son (whose own kidneys work fine). Commenting on her surgeries, Dolly remarks that "Some of them died on me but I didn't take it to heart; after all, what were a few [German] babies compared to . . . I left them lying there with their guts spilling out and took a coffee break" (54). Whose life is worth preserving? Only Son's. Dolly describes injecting people with morphine in her guise as a physician in order to save her unwitting and often perfectly healthy "patients." Describing herself as Doctor Dolly, she declares that everyone in Dolly City is in desperate need of her: "'You're sick' I screamed in the streets of Dolly City. Let me heal you . . . I stopped passers-by; I asked them to let me operate on them because they were very sick" (73).

On her mad healing rampage, no one and nothing is safe from Dolly's evangelical fervor. Stalking around the city with hypodermic needle in hand, Dolly injects all that she sees: "The cars had cancer too . . . I tried to help . . . the cripples, the welfare coupons, the purses and the cats . . . they were all very sick" (73). Dolly is a fatally self-deluded healer, and no object, whether animate or inanimate, is safe from her ministrations. And if she can't cure

you, she will kill you. Speaking with a woman who describes cancer metasta-
sizing inside her, Doctor Dolly shoots her after asking "Would you like me to
turn you into a take-away?" (117). Destroying at will is her modus operandi,
random death the result of ferocious and bogus ministrations.

Seeing the surrounding world as desperately sick is essential for how
Dolly organizes reality. Only disease engages her. A state of stasis is unbearable, and she loses interest. Continually cutting up Son to look for cancer is
the most persistent metaphor for Dolly's incurable search to find only what is
wrong, her unremitting need to unsettle that which might be at ease. "When I
wasn't rummaging in [Son's] insides, I didn't relate to him at all" (65). Her
addiction to disequilibrium is literally and figuratively insatiable, spurring
her into manic action. In the face of overwhelming odds from the spreading
of [imagined] malevolent cancers, Dolly insists she only wants to heal Dolly
City's poor wretches. But her healing is destruction described as its opposite,
not unlike Israel's use of euphemisms to name what everyone else calls
occupation. Dolly would no doubt call the checkpoints comfort stations.

Out to save the world, unstoppable in her crusade, Dolly proclaims she
will halt the terrifying spread of this horrible disease no matter how painful
the treatment. Cutting up and injecting anyone and everything in a frenzied
attempt to triumph over ubiquitous malignancy, she'll even minister to Arabs
from the Territories. Cancer is everywhere and enemies stalk all corners of
the country. No matter, for Dolly will aggressively destroy whatever hints at
being a danger. And she will, of course, leave behind a mess. At the risk of
belaboring the obvious and subtracting from the ferocious wit of Castel-
Bloom's metaphor, Israel/Dolly will destroy the world in order to save it.

The finest example of Dolly's manic power and the novel's ultimate in
mad symbolism occurs when Dolly draws a map of Israel on Son's back.
Using a knife, she traces an outline based on the land as described in the
Bible. The drops of blood arising from the carved river beds cause not anguish but delight, as Dolly rejoices in the irrevocable fact of the map cut into
the human flesh of her son. No one, she remarks, can mistake the reality
carved into this human body: "I took a knife and began cutting here and
there. Drops of blood began welling up in the riverbeds . . . the map of the
Land of Israel amateurishly sketched on my son's back gave me a frisson of
delight. My baby screamed in pain but I stood firm . . . it was the map of the
Land of Israel; nobody could mistake it" (44).

In a nutshell, here is a virtual summary of Dolly's Israel. It doesn't matter
that the map was partially carved out of the flesh of another. That map is now
indisputable. And no matter that the pain associated with its creation continues to anguish. It is now an irreversible artifact. Facts on the ground have
been established. Hearing her baby scream doesn't interfere with Dolly's
sense that this pain is worth inflicting, no matter the cost to self or other. As
Dolly reminds us, "nobody could mistake" what is carved out in blood and

flesh. The sword makes the map, again, and again, and again. No amount of wailing can stop the process.

Whatever she is going after, Castel-Bloom's ability to maintain an exquisite level of verbal jousting and metaphorical exaggeration is extraordinary. Satire is humor that is often savage, masking—or letting loose—a fierce anger at human and institutional folly. It also may imply moral judgments made with the idea of suggesting urgent realignments. Castel-Bloom is satirizing an Israel run amuck, destroying parts of itself while simultaneously demonizing others. Implicit in her coruscating censure is the need for Israel to do something, before it is too late, to fix an untenable state of affairs.

One may discern in *Dolly City* an underlying rage, anger brought to heel by a sensibility skilled in rendering absurd that which is odious and infuriating. The situation in Israel is so dire that attempts to make sense of what's happening often feel overwhelming and well-nigh impossible. To put it in a less genteel way, what's going on in Israel at this point in its history is enough to drive a person to a Dolly-like state of craziness.

NO PLACE TO GO (*HUMAN PARTS*)

Castel-Bloom's second book, *Human Parts*, was published in 2003, six years after *Dolly City*. Like its predecessor, it is also bitingly satirical. But it is less raw than *Dolly City*, and people and events are presented with more realism. In this fictional world, an unrelenting gray despair is less an opportunity for mockery than responses compounded of resignation and a bitter acknowledgement of futility. *Dolly City* is an outrageous fable lightened by zaniness. The crazy inventiveness of its universe brings in lots of surrealist light. In contrast, *Human Parts*' dystopian world has settled into patterns that are boringly intractable. All vitality has been drained away. As bad as things are, the situation is only likely to get worse. The matter-of-factness characterizing people and events in *Human Parts* grounds them in the quotidian. It's all too easy to imagine that an oppressive reality is here to stay, familiar in its despair.

From the first sentence, readers are introduced to a grim situation: "It was an exceptional winter. Not at all like the brief winter the inhabitants of Israel were used to . . . [it brought] a message of drought, hunger, poverty, unemployment, recession, boredom, despair and existential panic" (3). At once we know that we are in the real country of Israel, and that times are bad in a way they have not been before. In *Dolly City*, the first thing we learn is that Dolly's goldfish died. That was a small personal loss, something that could happen to anyone in any locale. The specificity of place throughout Dolly's adventures is never spelled out clearly, only allegorically, and the place name of the major Israeli city where the action unfolds is fictitious albeit recognizable.

On the other hand, *Human Parts* portrays terrible weather and catastrophic social conditions in specific Israeli locales. The first few pages go on to describe flooding on a scale that invokes Noah and his Ark with "Raindrops the size of olives . . . [and] an almost constant drizzle that left the ground permanently wet" (4). This kind of hyperbole appears frequently in *Human Parts*, but the absurdity never reaches the heights (or depths) of *Dolly City*. The exaggerations are grounded in reality with more recognizable phenomena. The impact of events is often less dramatic than the wildness and inventiveness of occurrences in Dolly's world, but is equally powerful in evoking a country greatly ill at ease with itself.

The omniscient narrator of *Human Parts* relates that "Owing to the heavy snow drifts, trees planted by the pioneers early in the previous century fell to the ground" (5). Not only is the terrible weather unprecedented in Israeli history, but it creates conditions which topple vegetation put in place by the country's earliest settlers. Those who came to Israel during the first settlement wave in the early twentieth century occupy a hallowed place in the mind of contemporary Israelis. The word "pioneer" connotes fearlessness, a willingness to face any and all obstacles in pursuit of the goal of conquering a wild place—never mind that others had already made a life there. When something created by these heroes is destroyed, it is considered an erosion of a sacred legacy. Castel-Bloom is once again in the myth-wrecking business, alerting us that things are not what they once were—or what they were once thought to be. A fundamental shift in that most universal condition, the weather, is only the beginning of a series of unravelings. Also coming apart are the early myths continually evoked though now out-of-date.

Just when one thinks this will be a more or less straightforward narrative, the biting wit of Castel-Bloom emerges. Readers learn that:

> [W]eather forecasters . . . became celebrities . . . frequently [taking] part in game shows. . . . One forecaster won half a million shekels for the correct answer to the question, what is the life expectancy of an Asiatic lion? The next day he was fatally injured in a shooting attack when he was on his way to Ikea to buy new furniture for his home. (5)

The absurdity here is slightly muted, but not to be missed. How ridiculous but true that weather forecasters have become celebrities, and what ignominious ends await such foolish people. Nowadays all kinds of circumstances make for celebrity; entire television channels are devoted to the weather and reality-show contestants expose personal inanities to make a fortune. Sometimes it is hard to see the satire in *Human Parts* because so much of today's world has made real what previously would have been incredible. The overarching theme of this novel is that current Israeli culture is both absurd and doomed. Television programming mirrors a national discourse dumbed down and manipulative. It is a discourse which encourages displacement of attention to critical matters by offering mindless diversion.

Castel-Bloom targets Israeli reality television in all its cringe-worthy pandering to the lowest common denominator and avoidance of serious issues by presenting cheap sentimental human drama: "The community channel . . . [presented] a touching human story of hardship—relatively refreshing in comparison to the grief and misery caused by the Arab terror" (10). This so-called Arab terror thrusts itself into the conversation of *Human Parts*, providing continuous background noise. Disregarded as an uncomfortable yet intractable situation, the ongoing conflict turns into another clichéd non-reality. While there are scattered references to a conflict casting an unresolved pall, the book's characters are not in the business of confronting or attempting to change it. Instead of making the country's ongoing state of bellicosity a subject of nuanced discourse, it is relegated to a situation not unlike the terrible weather. Everybody complains about it but no one does anything to change it.

The subject of this community-channel televised story is a poor family. It features a couple of appearances of the family's wife and mother, Kati, a cleaning woman. This star/victim is pulled into the world of sensational media, her pitiful personal story distracting from more urgent concerns. Kati and her family receive all kinds of goods and services as a result of her television appearances, but after a week,

> [T]he presenter of the morning show to which Kati had been invited, as the popular representative of poverty in Israel, announced that poverty was no longer the hot news it had been the week before . . . Kati, a media has-been, was thrown . . . into a taxi . . . The next day, when she reluctantly went back to cleaning the stairwells . . . nobody recognized her as the person who had appeared on television. (98–99, 105–6)

Sic gloria transit. Kati, symbol of Israel's downtrodden, has had her sixty seconds of fame. For that matter, poverty itself may now exit the stage and be dismissed from further consideration. Kati's situation is a glossed-over presentation of one family's dire straits, the details of which are exploited by a fickle and self-serving media establishment in order to serve a public eager for distraction. Stories of Kati and her like come and go. They are interchangable pathetic human detritus gawked at and gobbled up by an insatiable citizenry.

It is not only television that plays games with the public's emotions, particularly grief. In Israel, regular radio broadcasts are a staple of daily life and an hourly barometer of national concerns. Here's Castel-Bloom's mordantly witty description of radio stations choosing which music to accompany news of tragedies: "From ten dead and up, the radio networks switched to a far more serious mode, confined to Hebrew songs only . . . From twenty dead and up, they changed the format to Plan B, like hospitals on high alert. . . . Now, with only one man dead and one wounded woman . . . the radio stations went on broadcasting ordinary songs" (242–43). The public mood is manipulated by tunes and tales of woe, background cues to the human condition. Shall it be Mozart or Madonna? Radio producers will count the number of dead and then decide.

Kati's woes are one thread running through the book which is essentially a string of anecdotes about five or six families and what happens to them in their disintegrating country. The other major characters are Iris, a divorced mother of two; Adir, a wealthy Israeli and his Ethiopian-born girlfriend, Tasar, and Kati's husband Boaz. Their lives are intertwined mainly through coincidence and chance encounters. There is no attempt to present an in-depth look at any of the people, nor to explore their characters beyond a presentation of defining idiosyncrasies. They serve mainly as vehicles for examining the difficulties of modern-day Israel, pointing to how absurdly dysfunctional everything is. The novel's main character is the time and place in which these people live. What is most alive in *Human Parts* is the gray sadness of Israel, and the feeling that no forward movement is conceivable.

While some might read *Human Parts* as social realism, it is more accurate to recognize that in fact the Israeli world has become more Castel-Bloomian. The people and events in the Israel of her book are trapped. Highlighting prevailing pessimism, one character remarks that "Israel is one of the most depressing places in the world today" (209). For another person, "Life in Israel [is] unbearable. . . . He couldn't stand to see all this death around him anymore. He saw Israel as a big graveyard with enclaves of settlements in which people were still living, but they too would probably be dead soon" (202). Another character remarks that "In the streets, in the shopping malls, in the bus terminals, people tried to act as if they were carrying on with their lives as usual, but everyone knew that the situation was intolerable" (24-5).

Allusions to real-time stalemates reinforce the sense of hopelessness: "The peace process with the Palestinians, in all its phases, collapsed like one of the houses whose roof gave way under the weight of the snow" (5). A discussion of people killed or wounded by suicide bombers, the publicity these events generate, the reaction of the country's political leaders, and the military response to terrorist attacks follows. There is never a resolution nor a sense that the country's leaders have behaved wisely. Throughout the novel, references to externally inflicted catastrophes are described in terms alternately realistic and satirically exaggerated. Interleaving these styles makes room for Castel-Bloom to evoke actual situations the country faces while mocking the ineffective responses the crises elicit.

Catastrophes come from all kinds of sources: terrorism, the weather, virulent viral illnesses that kill many people, and less contagious but no less deadly bodily ills—as when one character dies of cardiac arrest in the hospital and another has a potentially fatal asthma attack. Another character cannot afford dental work and experiences herself in serious decay. On the positive side, the chaos of disease even transcends ancient enmities: "The flu also affected the inhabitants of the Palestinian Authority, and there, too, many people died. Sometimes the illness and the severe cold brought fighters on both sides to their knees, and created the illusion of a cease-fire" (23).

As with the fear of cancer and other diseases in *Dolly City*, there is a great deal of focus on the vulnerability of the human body, a continual link between human physical decay and death with larger issues of societal dysfunction. Calling the book *Human Parts* points the way towards these connections, suggesting a juxtaposition of bodies deteriorating in a nation also falling apart. Overwhelming despair pervades this novel, a sense of things going from bad to worse. The Israeli establishment uses the presence of external danger to excuse its failures to cope with the disastrous plight of its citizens. There is no foreseeable way out of the intractable political situation, and the response is a state of continuous fear compounded of rage and cynicism.

Castel-Bloom does not concern herself either with condemning the terrorists, glorifying Palestinian hopes, or arguing the need for a meaningful peace process. She concentrates on presenting the erosion of Israelis' lives in terms of how they respond to their bleak circumstances. Whether these responses make sense or are inevitable or absurd is for the reader to decide. One character sums up the ennui and despair in his reaction to the ongoing warfare between Israelis and Palestinians:

> He didn't have a solution of his own to the conflict and therefore he didn't interfere. . . . Not that he was indifferent, he just thought it would take years until this conflict was resolved. Maybe even a thousand. When he thought about it seriously, and he often thought about it seriously, he asked himself why the State of Israel didn't move itself to some deserted plain where there weren't any enemies, like one of the poles. (37)

Location, location, location. The establishment of Israel in a land already partially occupied by others, in a place short of water and long on disputation, is a question still posed in some quarters. While there is zero possibility of a change of venue, Castel-Bloom turns over this stone as well. If the land were elsewhere, might it avoid limitless pain? Perhaps Israel should not have come to this site, no matter that the Bible's surveyor pointed out where X marks the spot.

The established members of Israeli society are all part of the problem—ineffective but well meaning at best, stupidly self-important and superficial at worst. Israel's politicians are a prime target of Castel-Bloom's scorn. They are paralyzed with indecision, as unable to address the country's ills as anyone else. Israel's president is a kindly but ineffective figure whose main work appears to be paying condolence calls on victims of terrorist attacks: "he was obliged to make his way to the many funerals and to the hospitals in his limousine, driving for hours on end and taking naps between one funeral and the next" (100). The book ends with the president telling his driver to turn off the radio: "'Quiet, all I want is quiet. No music and no talking. Just quiet'" (249). He sits in the car gazing out and thinking of his daughter who is in her second year at Harvard, remembering the view from her Boston apartment.

This closing image intimates that the only way out is to leave the country and establish a life someplace else. Like all around him, the president is clueless about what preventive action might be taken to stop the destruction that arises from natural calamities like the weather and man-made catastrophes like the Israeli-Palestinian conflict. In fact, he was elected for fairly lame reasons: "in addition to the advantages of his appealing appearance and fine taste in clothes . . . the many people who favored his candidacy for the presidency added the fact that his roots were deeply planted in Jerusalem" (70–71). The good-looking homeboy is chosen, his looks and familiar background making for a nonthreatening choice of leader.

In fact, not only is the president unable to formulate an effective response to massive disorders; no one in power has a clue:

> The Politicians . . . were at a loss in the face of the increasing escalation. In order to make it easier for themselves and the public at large to grasp the changing reality, they invented an imaginary staircase, and dubbed every additional deterioration in the situation or every terrorist attack that was worse than the one before it as a 'step up.' (7)

This foolish, empty image is constructed by politicians to further obfuscate the roots of the Palestinian-Israeli conflict and to distract people from giving serious thought to alternatives. Deterioration is envisioned as an inevitable process where one simply watches the calamities mount. No one is invited to consider what might be done to dismantle this stairway of death. The shifting of responsibility to factors outside the control of those involved becomes a modus operandi for not searching out ways to resolve the impasse. Whether it's unemployment or terrorism, ongoing war or bad weather, it's acts of God that dictate circumstances. Castel-Bloom lays out the folly of a willed sense on the part of citizens and their government leaders that they can do nothing to change the circumstances in which they are living and in which they and others are dying.

Any attempt to escape danger is doomed. Kati's husband Boaz gets lost trying to get out of Jerusalem and go back home to Tel Aviv: "He didn't want to live in a place [Jerusalem] that three religions were fighting over . . . as he started the car . . . A cold sweat broke out on his back . . . in a terrorist ambush . . . Boaz died instantly" (232, 236–37). His random death is pointless as well as sad. Boaz just wanted to get away from the dangers of Jerusalem and find his way to safer Tel Aviv. But trapped by chance, he is killed in the city which is Castel-Bloom's ultimate site for mayhem.

Compounding all the misery is a sense of national isolation, a feeling that the country is in a universe increasingly cut off from the outside world. Israel often behaves as if it is alone in the world confronting implacable enemies, often positioning itself as David versus Goliath—this in spite of the fact that its military is among the world's most powerful and that it has repeatedly triumphed over those who sought to do it harm. The inhabitants in *Human Parts* watch as the outside world stays away:

> [T]ourism was dealt a crushing blow. Many flights to Israel were cancelled. Foreign airlines were worried about the safety of their crews and . . . made sure that [the crews] would leave the country before darkness descended. The air crews were afraid to sleep in Israel. Even the town of Eilat and its surroundings, which had always attracted tourists during the winter season, turned into a ghost town. (22)

The book is a litany of despair, and the pervading sense is of individuals longing to be elsewhere. This is the ultimate irony. After all the centuries of suffering and wandering and longing to come home to Israel, this is a place of misery. The president envisions himself walking down a Boston street with his wife and daughter considering "whether to rent or buy" (249). His driver watches a bird circling overhead and remarks "There's nothing here even for the birds. . . . So who is there something here for?" (248). Who indeed.

Both *Dolly City* and *Human Parts* are discomforting portraits of a world severely out of joint, with little hope of redemption. In *Human Parts* events occur in clearly defined towns and even familiar streets in Jerusalem and Tel Aviv. Characters are recognizable as actual people. Some may find this more realistic dystopian novel disturbing in ways that the totally unrealistic *Dolly City* is not. But however one prefers to take one's despair at current Israeli quandaries—whether straight up or with a shot of bracing nuttiness—Castel-Bloom is an invaluable voice in the conversation about the country. She explores the idealized dream of a holy land transformed into a present-day sea of problems. As with many other nations, the founding vision of Israel began as a shining ideal. The nation was conceived as a homeland for Jews after millions of deaths in concentration camps and the refusal of almost every country to admit Jewish refugees. It was founded with the idea of being a place of justice and equality for Arabs as well as Jews. Even with mounting evidence to the contrary, many still persist in idealizing the country as a holy land exempt from the limitations of a modern nation-state. But that fantasy grows more faint as Israel, now well past its infancy, persists in maintaining policies increasingly seen as unsustainable.

Israel is not the only country to struggle with competing narratives about what its identity should be and how it can maintain itself as whole, while yet open to the legitimate claims of others. Jerusalem is not the only so-called holy city in today's world; one may look to Karbala or Mecca for helpful comparisons. Israel remains prominent in global discourse partly because of its location. Alas, it also commands attention because it is the State of the Jews, and Jew-hatred is a constant in world history.

Nevertheless, writers like Castel-Bloom may move us to ask what it might take for this particular country and its worldwide supporters to move towards justice. Dolly's last words are "My heart pounded in my breast with excitement and my brain danced . . . I knew that, after everything I'd done to [Son], a bullet or a knife in the back was nothing he couldn't cope with" (182). Perhaps the bloodlust in her final crazy boast may goad us to consider what it would take to end the dance of excitement that comes from violence, to put aside bullets and knives in a search for the quiet of peace in Dolly's fractured country.

NOTES

1. At the time of this writing, Israel's Prime Minister, Benjamin Netanyahu, referred to this biblical "promise" (and used the ancient names Judea and Samaria in reference to the disputed Palestinian territories in the West Bank) telling the U.S. Congress, May 24, 2011, "In Judea-Samaria, the Jewish people are not foreign occupiers. This is the land of our forefathers—the land of Israel—to which Abraham brought the idea of one God, where David set out to confront Goliath, and where Isaiah saw a vision of eternal peace. . . . No distortion of history can deny the 4,000-year-old bond between the Jewish people and the Jewish land."

2. Guttman, Nathan (2010). "With 700,000 supporters, CUFI [Christians United for Israel] is the largest pro-Israel organization in America. . . . Pro-Israel activists point to CUFI's potential reservoir of 50 million to 70 million evangelical Americans as Israel's best chance to ensure lasting support within the United States." And "Last year the group (CUFI) distributed . . . more than $8 million to Israeli and Jewish organizations, according to CUFI."

3. Charles S. Liebman and Eli'ezer Don-Yiha (1982), point to ways key factions of early Zionism appropriated religious Judaism to serve their ends: "Zionist-socialism was a religious surrogate . . . its radical secularism . . . led it to absorb the symbols and values of the tradition selectively and to reformulate the tradition in its own spirit" (30) and "Jewish nationalists, represented primarily by secular Zionism, sought subsitutes for religious symbols . . . a vision of sociopolitcal redemption to be realized by national rather than supernatural means" (25).

4. As Gershom Gorenberg (2011) states, "The purpose of settlement . . . had been to create facts that would determine the final status of the land, to sculpt the political reality before negotiations ever got under way. . . . By the summer of 2005 . . . nearly 250,000 Israelis [were] living in 125 officially recognized West Bank settlements. Another 180,000 lived in the annexed areas of East Jerusaem—land regarded . . . by other countries as being under occupation. In the Golan Heights . . . 16,000 Israelis lived in 32 settlements" (364).

5. For instance, the 1999 platform of the Likud party flatly states: "Jerusalem is the eternal, united capital of the State of Israel and only of Israel. The government will flatly reject Palestinian proposals to divide Jerusalem, including the plan to divide the city presented to the

Knesset by the Arab factions and supported by many members of Labor and Meretz. The government firmly rejects attempts of various sources in the world, some anti-Semitic in origin, to question Jerusalem's status as Israel's capital, and the 3,000-year-old special connection between the Jewish people and its capital. To ensure this, the government will continue the firm policies it has adopted until now." Online: knesset.gov.il. Furthermore, this position is held by the majority of the Israeli population, as surveyed by the BESA Center in March 2008: "A large majority of the total sample (62%) were against Jerusalem's status being discussed within the framework of negotiations for peace arrangements with the Palestinians. . . . Most respondents out of the total sample (58%) thought that Israel should not, in principle, agree to divide Jerusalem between itself and the Palestinians in return for a final status agreement with the Palestinians and a declaration calling an end to the conflict with the Arab world."

6. Israel's borders are still not definitively settled. The borderlines between Syria and the Palestinian Territories remain fluid. Gershon Gorenberg (2011) writes "The rule of law . . . is essential to a democratic state. By increments, the settlement project hollowed out the rule of law . . . Settlements erased Israel's border, or created several" (89).

7. Neil Caplan (2010) describes the clash of irreconcilable narratives: "Intangible issues involving psychology, myths, sterotyping, and contested narratives are . . . often existential issues . . . and these are the issues that are the most difficult to resolve" (29).

Chapter Three

God, Text and the Holy Land

Michal Govrin

To die like Rachel
When the soul shudders like a bird
Wants to break free . . .
To die like Rachel,
That's what I want.
(Ravikovich 2009)

Perceptions of God and the sacred as expressed in text remain part of Jewish discourse either as positive or negative influences, depending on one's point of view. In today's Israel, tensions between secular Jews and those who hold a more religionist perspective are causes of increasing division and bitterness. Religious orthodoxy has moved to the center of Israel's ideological agenda, with fundamentalist Jews a major force in determining public policy. Fundamentalist readings of text have become more narrow and also increasingly acceptable. Questions about how democracy in Israel can thrive when theocratic forces gain ascendancy is an issue likely to become increasingly relevant.

Core notions as to what constitutes the Jewish people have always been intimately linked to how text is interpreted. The term "text" encompasses a wide variety of materials pertaining to the study of Hebrew writings, beginning with the Hebrew Bible. Text refers to that document as well as the literally innumerable commentaries authored over the centuries up to and including the present day. Not for nothing are Jews called the People of the Book. The parameters of the Jewish world are laid out in constant dialogue with critical exegesis, both ancient and contemporary. Engagement with these sources involves grappling with the notion of authority in general and

God in particular, along with an endless number of other concerns including those related to the role of women and their bodies.

Besides text demarcated in the centuries-old Hebrew Bible, there is also commentary as spelled out in early Zionist writings envisioning what kind of nation Israel was to be. Israel's pioneer settlers wove a compelling vision of their homeland, a place where Jews would hold sway over the nation that belonged to them. For today's Israeli, the early pioneers who settled Israel both before and after it became a Jewish state retain a hallowed role in the nation's mythology. What the pioneers said and did is invoked with the same fervor with which U.S. citizens recall the Founding Fathers. In both countries, it is the fathers and never the mothers whose long-ago dreams remain part of each nation's subconscious self-definition.

Inherent in Zionist writings is the privileging of male roles over that of female. The early Jewish feminist scholar Judith Plaskow (1990) noted "The Labor Zionist movement . . . subordinated women's emancipation to the overriding project of establishing a Jewish home. . . . With the establishment of the state of Israel in 1948, important new factors came into play that served to consolidate and intensify sexual inequality" (110). This inequality is still present in the ways women's role in relation to God and the sacred is defined today. [1] [2]

The entrenchment of gender inequality in religious realms has hardened over time. Israel's Ministry of Religious Affairs, an agency notable in itself for its existence as part of the State apparatus, recognizes two chief rabbis who are the supreme authority for all matters of religious law throughout the country. A Religious Council in each community oversees all aspects of religious observance. These one hundred seventy bodies oversee activities in the private sphere, all ensuring that males are given first priority in any matter of domestic importance. Beyond the confines of the home, in some Israeli settings ultra-Orthodox authorities also adjudicate such issues as what a woman may wear in public and where she may sit on a bus.

Because private life in Israel is completely governed by traditional text-based law as interpreted by rabbinic authorities, marriage and divorce can only take place under rabbinically determined guidelines. The rabbis who determine the law are male and Orthodox. Ruth Halperin-Kaddari (2004), a critic of Israeli family, law notes

> [Israeli law] conceives marriage as a one-sided transaction in which the man betroths the woman and not the opposite, which sanctions inequality and discrimination regarding spousal obligations and rights towards each other during the course of marriage, and sanctions harsh limitations over the process of divorce and inequalities with respect to it, to the detriment of women. (228)

> The status of men and women during marriage is far from equal. As a traditional patriarchal system, Jewish law strongly adheres to strict gender roles in the family. (236)

While the weight of male dominated religiosity is experienced by all Israeli women, it can be particularly cruel to those women for whom an ongoing search for God is a preoccupation. Their struggle to mold lives based on textual understandings of the sacred (including but not limited to God) is confounded by the fact that religious authority in Israel, as in many other places, is overwhelmingly male-defined. Women are continually told they must conform to a male religious framework as this is the way God intended the world to be. While many women choose to sidestep the belief-related implications of this emotional briar patch, others' religious impulses lead to constant battle with the outside religious world and with their own inner turmoil. They struggle to find themselves in the text, to read women into sacred spaces where only a male presence is visible.

Michal Govrin's work brilliantly examines the nature of religiosity and the influence of masculinized text in the lives of women in today's Israel. Her two books, *The Name* and *Snapshots*, present heroines attempting to come to terms with their understanding of God, of text, of authority, of themselves—and in particular, their physical selves—in an Israeli religious universe formed and governed by men. In *The Name,* the narrator's religious impulse ends in suicide. Amalia's passionate search for a connection to her ever-present Jewish God leads her to conclude that she is irredeemably contaminated. In *Snapshots*, Govrin's heroine attempts to reorder a masculine text-based world by tackling traditional authority with tools of architecture, transforming space as a road to the divine. Ilana's compelling text is that of the early Zionists more than that of ancient sages. But for both women, the stakes are enormous as they find themselves living within textual interpretations which place them in a one-down position.

Govrin's books compel feminist readings as their female protagonists struggle to locate meaning in traditional realms where parameters are set by men. Each woman strives, often by means of her body, to mirror existential truths. Attempting to delineate themselves, both women demonstrate abstract ideas expressed through the female body. Intense sexuality becomes a primary vehicle for making meaning in the world. Sexuality is a chosen tool for connecting—to self, to others, to transcendence. Notably, neither of Govrin's women is prepared to repudiate the [male] textual sources that determine the universes they inhabit and are desperately trying to navigate. Their tensions play out between conventional received truths they have internalized and those that emerge from their own experiences. Ultimately, there is no reconciliation. In the end, their embodied readings of text lead to destruction.

The backdrop for Govrin's first novel, *The Name*, is the world of the so-called *Haredi*.[3] These are the most fundamentalist Jewish religionists. They are thought to represent approximately ten percent of the current Israeli population, but some demographers see them rapidly increasing in the next decade.[4]

Haredim live in enclosed, isolated communities where their interpretation of biblical law is strict, with an insistence that only unquestioning adherence to basic masculinized tenets is acceptable. There can be no deviation from their proscribed biblical way, and that avenue is suffocatingly narrow in how women's roles are defined. Sadly, incidents demonstrating some *Haredim*'s profound contempt for women may be found in descriptions of females being physically attacked for transgressing norms of modesty.

While *Haredim* do not represent all of Israel's religious communities, and while there are distinctions between ultra-Orthodox groups, the position of the theological right as a societal force is strong. Its position is buttressed by the reality that Israeli family law is determined by the Orthodox Rabbinic Councils. Strictly interpreted religious-based law, not law based on secular precepts, governs all domestic matters. The *Haredi* influence is spreading into institutions such as the Israeli military, where the presence of ultra-Orthodox adherents is increasing. A recent book by Gershom Gorenberg (2011), arguing the need for societal shifts in Israel, notes "since 2005, the army's dependence on soldiers coming out of the Orthodox academies . . . and other *yeshivot* (seminaries for training of Orthodox rabbis) aligned with the theological right has increased" (153). Ultra-Orthodox schools teach text based on strict ideological interpretations. In the militantly nationalist settler movement, "the most ideologically committed settlers have been religious Zionists—and the government's support for settlement has fostered the transformation of religious Zionism into a movement of the radical right" (8). Religionists refer to the disputed territories as Judea and Samaria, their biblical names, rather than as the West Bank. Because ultra-Orthodox Judaism's influence is on the rise in Israel, it is imperative to try to comprehend something about its wellsprings.

Govrin (1998) understands fervent religiosity. She has a deep, wide-ranging understanding of traditional texts, and her impressive knowledge grounds her novels in ancient sources. Govrin herself states that "*The Name* was written in dialogue with voices that emerged from the pages of the 'Jewish book'" (Acknowledgments). The book's very title is a recognition that great care is taken when referring to the Hebrew God, as the various names for God are often not directly invoked. When identifying God, the phrase *Hashem* (the name) is frequently used. Her writings highlight the added theocratic edge that comes from living in a designated holy land, source of Judeo-Christian-Muslim belief. Whether or not one is a believer, Govrin demonstrates how the longing for connection with age-old textual sources can be as compelling as any biological imperative. Evoking the power of holy writ, she makes clear its majestic, literally awe-ful power. At the same time, Govrin suggests new metaphors from a feminist perspective for envisioning the divine and imagining how that might change Israel.

AND GOD DESTROYED WOMAN (*THE NAME*)

An intense search for God, and the destruction that ensues from it, is at the heart of *The Name*'s narrative. The novel is the story of a young woman, Amalia, who seeks to fuse herself with God through living in adherence to the precepts found in an Israeli ultra-Orthodox (*Haredi*) Jewish interpretation of traditional text. What specifically shapes Amalia's interior landscape? Longing for God, secular Amalia arrives in Jerusalem where she enters a girl's school to study Orthodox Judaism. With such a step, she enters into a strict, fundamentalist Jewish sphere and begins to live an existence dictated by its (male) religious authorities. This religious world determines her sense of who she is, a self-image in which she comes to see herself as unworthy, defiled and sinful. The battleground on which her self-hating feelings play out is Amalia's body. It is by means of those two old verities—sex and death—that Amalia tries both to eradicate coruscating feelings of unworthiness and to find her way to divine connection. The boundaries of the battles she wages are determined by attempts to reorder text through her own writing and through an understanding of God based on a physical means of divine union.

Finding ways of expressing the materiality of her God returns Amalia to the notion that God is first to be located in the word. Throughout this very long book, she never stops talking to her divine lover using the language of traditional text. A ceaseless flow of words spills forth as Amalia prepares to join her beloved God in the final act of sacrificing herself through suicide. This stunning truth underlies everything we read: from page one onward, this young woman is planning to kill herself so that she and God will become one. Her imminent suicide is suggested very subtly, and it may take repeated readings to be certain of it. This understatement is the perfect literary device; the reader is forced to pay close attention to Amalia's interior dialogue—to her text—to figure out where she's going. Her self-inflicted death is based on words, words, words—all of which come out of her (mis)reading of what this masculinized god would have her, a mere woman, do.

To a secular reader, the overweening yearning for connection to God can strain credulity. But Govrin's passionate invocation of the efficacy of a traditional deity is worth any effort it takes to enter into her fictive world. For individuals and communities who cry out for a transcendent reality, the longing for God is intense. No amount of so-called rational thinking can dislodge this yearning. Govrin's creation of a character who literally embodies an insatiable longing for a divine connection gives insight into the power of such desire. Amalia's Jewish divinity springs to life through ancient Hebrew texts, objects, customs, rituals. These things form a complex web of associations meant to describe, celebrate, importune and dialogue with that Creator or that man-made creation (depending on your point of view). Many Amalias live in Israel as elsewhere, struggling for legitimacy in religious worlds too often dominated by men whose unwavering belief in a rigid version of a Jewish god justifies shoving women to the fringes of their putative holy world.

Watching Amalia hurtle towards her self-chosen end, riding on a wave of words, is to witness a journey of disturbing intensity as Govrin infuses her narrative with a frenzied, hysterical edge. Two biblical passages bracket Amalia's entire existence. Here's Amalia, at the beginning of the novel, importuning God: "May it be Your will . . . Holy Name, my God and God of my fathers . . . [that] I be cleansed and sanctified with the Holiness of Above. . . . And may You want me" (3-4). And here she is on the last page concluding her story—and her young life—with these words: "The Lord gives and the Lord takes away; blessed be the Name of the Lord" (438). The events that take place between the invocations of these two textual references make us partners in an extraordinary interior journey as harrowing as any physical odyssey.

The desire to have God want her is a striking insight into the sexuality that underlies Amalia's journey for divine fusion. For along with searching for connection to God through words, Amalia yearns for a physical consummation. Her spiritual desire carries a powerful erotic charge. Ultimately, suicide becomes the means through which her body is joined to God, death ensuring the ultimate passionate embrace. Amalia's body is the arena upon which feelings, desires and conflicts are acted out. Everything of importance to her—both positive and negative—is literally embodied as well as expressed through textual metaphor. Sexuality is her road to salvation, the main pathway to the divine, not to sexual gratification *per se.*

Her conversations with God are suffused with sexual longing, and the trajectory of her emotions follows the course of love affairs the world over (though most affairs are surely less ephemeral than this one). Imagining herself with her beloved, she envisions a direct physical commingling with no intermediary between herself and God as she writes, "And the body is already burning in Your fire" (4). Time after time, Amalia's unvarnished desire for sexual union with God (which she sees as essential to her redemption) is expressed: "[L]ess than thirty days until I cling to your kiss" (105). "I shall give myself to You an unblemished offering. I shall come to a covenant with You purely . . . there is no redemption except in love of You" (155-156). "You [chose] me, a bride of blood to You, me, black as a raven, Your salvation, I . . . shall lie in Your bosom with my dry body that my Lord the King may get heat . . . I shall give myself to You with devotion, and You shall consecrate me in Your sweetness and You shall embrace me to Your bosom, and than I shall rouse Your desire towards me" (246-247). "Is that how we shall whisper, embracing each other, when You will sanctify me and I shall give myself to You . . . when You will hold the back of my neck, when we shall cling tongue to tongue, when You will lap my insides. And You will want me, a full offering" (337).

Here is a woman imagining, to put it mildly, a torrid love affair with God. The sexual component is undisguised, a means towards transecting boundaries. But there is also something fundamentally feminist, subversive and life-affirming in this sexual yearning if one considers theologian Rachel Adler's suggestion that " something in God in seeking its human mirror . . . [it] is as it were, God's sexuality" (118). The search may involve language as a way of navigating the distance that exists between that which is embodied and that which is incapable of being expressed. Amalia strains to join her body with that which is unattainable, her hot pursuit of divine lover spelled out in metaphor after metaphor. Her fevered language expresses desire to link with a sexualized divinity and to find in that union a yoking of body and soul with that which can never be materialized but is no less real.

This bliss of female-imagined divine consummation, however, is joined to its opposite: self loathing. Amalia's negativity and ultimately suicidal feelings arise within the context of a Jerusalem where religiosity for many men can be a scene of unbridled celebration mixed in with strong elements of lewd sexuality. But for women, this sexuality is a sin and an abomination. Rabbi Avuya Aserak, a male religious authority with whom she interacts, is the quintessence of religious fervor run amok. In his fierce sexual feelings for God and [wo]man, Rabbi Avuya Aserak sows enormous chaos. Amalia is introduced to him by Isaiah, the innocent young man who has been chosen by religious authorities to be her husband. Isaiah frequently makes his way to Aserak's quarters, where worship is often tumultuous:

> The students crowded together, pulling the benches under them tumultuously, raising their flashing faces towards the rabbi, who was banging his fist on the table, gripped by a profound shaking, his head swaying . . . And once again there was nothing for a moment but the noise of excitement . . . [Rabbi Aserak] . . . gathering around the curls of his beard splattered with the illuminated saliva, his ancient face blinded in the strength of the vow. The smoothness of his forehead covered with drops of sweat. (293-294)

> The pillar of voices ascended from the white swayings of the rabbi's body . . . winding in the heat permeating the room, drawing over the pungent body odors . . . it was impossible to distinguish the rabbi's chanting from the voices

of the congregation or the excited shrieks . . . or the words of the chanting of
the young woman next to you who shouted at the top of her lungs. (298-299)

This is religious worship as an ecstatic, frenzied, hysterical male rite. Its
strong undercurrent of eroticism plays out in the tumult of a near-orgiastic
celebration. Worship at the rabbi's is the coming to life of a male-embodied
text. The God-seeking Amalia finds herself pulled into this orbit as Rabbi
Aserak ogles and eventually copulates with her. She is distressed at his focus
on her, but Amalia also sees it as a message that she has been specially
chosen. Left alone with the rabbi, Amalia is propelled towards consummation, telling herself, "for the holy rabbi had chosen you, and how could you
reject his call? For he promised that after the torments, you would reach
salvation. . . . You followed him without any questions" (125).

It's a powerful scene of seduction, fueled by the young woman's hunger
for sacred connection and the rabbi's ruthless exploitation of her needs. Note
that the "you" addressed here is Amalia herself. Another sign of internal
splitting is addressing herself in the third person which she does frequently.
Rabbi Aserak lives in an almost continuous state of hyper-sexuality. In press-
ing Amalia towards intercourse, he works to satisfy a carnal hunger that
knows no boundaries. But the rabbi's hold on her springs from Amalia's self-
loathing. Amalia's body is a source of impurity to her, and she continually
seeks to transform her physicality. Picking up on her self-loathing, the rabbi
makes an easy conquest. Rabbi Aserak insists that sex with him will lift
Amalia out of defilement, cleansing her. He uses words grounded in textual
sources that speak directly to Amalia's perverse sense that she is deeply
repugnant to her god. As she copulates with him, Amalia reasons with herself
(again, she is the "you" being addressed):

> "[Y]ou have the power to raise sin to holiness. You . . . who sucks your life
> from the destruction . . . only real martyrdom, only the death of the soul for the
> sake of holiness can break open the blood of the mother giving birth . . . only
> the rabbi understood that you sank in sin in order to torment yourself with the
> torments of destruction, to know by yourself the real holy death, so that from
> sin fire will arise and sear together in repentance of salvation . . . he leaned
> over and whispered . . . it is not only your soul you will repair but also the
> souls of the dead . . . no one ever promised you as he did that from the root of
> the dread you would find salvation (122).

Amalia comes to accept that by having sex with this rabbi, she who lives in
the detritus of sin may be saved. And not only she will be saved; those she
has lost will also be redeemed. The rabbi's distorted, manipulative and de-
grading imagery is terrible in and of itself. Equally sad is that his words sum
up Amalia's internalized sense of self. Her inexorable progress towards self-
destruction is hastened by this exemplar of the religious world encouraging

the belief that her very existence is a source of the unholy. The rabbi's words are instruments of destruction for this pious, grieving young woman as he unerringly inflames all of her wounds. She is seduced both by the man himself and by what he as a rabbi represents: a socially sanctioned conduit for God.

This evocation of rabbinic power is a stark reminder of the influence that can come from perverted religious authority. It's also a comment on "The association of women with sexuality and female sexuality with God, connect[ing] God to an ethic of sexual intemperance, potentially wreaking havoc with an ethic of control" (Plaskow 1990, 188). Any changes in the ethic of control threaten to disturb the whole system of religiosity held together by a complex web of symbolic associations. It is the rabbi whose sexual practices bespeak sexual intemperance, but it is the woman Amalia who will be condemned for setting them off.

Traditional conceptions of God preclude the presence of sexuality of any kind—and most particularly any form of a feminine sexuality. Chaos will follow when sexuality is introduced into notions of what is holy, disturbing not only that which is sacred but upsetting the whole social order. If feminine sexuality is taken seriously, it undermines not only the traditional view of God but may inflict serious damage to the way normative cultural behavior is defined. Therefore, the potential for a profound change in religious metaphor—and ultimately reality—comes from the likes of Amalia who revels in such a highly sexual interaction with the divine. Reframing traditional religion to make a genuine place for women's perspective is to risk losing the certainty of a world constructed by men.

Amalia's sexuality is also a powerful exemplar of other aspects of feminism in conflict with the male world where women are not entitled to be included within the world of defining religious narratives. Describing the roles assigned to women by those who choose a masculinist, traditional reading of text, theologian Rachel Adler (1998) writes of the purported opposition between women and sacred text in traditional temptation narratives where "Women are the source of the life of the body—and hence of death. Holy text is a source of eternal life. A good woman, one who accepts her proper role . . . assigns her claim to visibility in deference to the superior claim of holy text. . . . A bad woman is one who makes herself a rival of the text" (11).

Adler's distinctions help in understanding how profoundly Amalia has internalized the worldview in which the way she lives her God-seeking life defines her in countless ways as a "bad woman." She lives in a world where men own the text, and she as a woman is marginal. No matter how hard she tries to serve God; no matter how much knowledge she has of Jewish sources; no matter how intense is her desire for holiness—she just doesn't count as a man would. Even her insistence on grounding her God-quest in textual sources is in and of itself transgressive. Setting herself up as someone worthy of divine conversation makes her, in Adler's words, "a rival of the text." This rivalry is unacceptable in a religious world where men alone are seen as the only legitimate purveyors of interpretation.

Not only are women to be invisible; they are also to be classified in terms of dualisms in which man is infinitely superior and woman inferior. As Adler points out, "Heaven and earth, light and darkness, spirit and body, cleanliness and filth, good and evil, freedom and slavery all are made to mirror the estrangement of patriarchal man from the woman he has cast out" (Adler 1998, 112).

Adler's dualisms are surely embodied in an Amalia who sees herself as "dark, filthy, evil." She is neither worthy of respect nor even worthy of life. Nothing she does has positive consequences; worse, all she does is impure. Therefore, with a terrible and relentless logic, self- annihilation offers meaning in a world stripped of other possibilities for holiness.

Before the final abandonment of her body to self-inflicted death, Amalia has allowed herself to be sexually exploited. Such a loathsome body—her own—deserves to be degraded as much as possible. In another stunning scene of self-loathing, Amalia describes rubbing filth into her scalp: "My hair was filthy with the dirt dripping grease and motor oil. That movement of scattering on the hair the defilement of the city absorbed in the dirt seemed like madness to me. And yet I went on crumbling, dirt on dirt" (Govrin 1998, 311).

Describing the placing of soiled earth (earth which is the ground of Jerusalem) as an act of putting "dirt on dirt" is the apotheosis of self-degradation. Compared to this, Amalia's readying of herself for impending suicide has an air of cleansing. Her ritualized preparations for death involve acts of washing and anointing her body in preparation for the end. These loving acts of self-care stand in marked contrast to the careless self-hatred she exhibits earlier. It is ironic that only in preparing for death does this tormented young woman come close to seeing her body as an object worthy of tenderness.

Accepting her fundamental inferiority, seeing herself as an unworthy dark force, it is clear that Amalia has internalized the values of her oppressive world making them part of her very being. Sadly, it is not only the men who reinforce this and add to despairing isolation. The women within this Jerusalem *Haredi* universe are part of the same system of control, their physical selves in thrall to male-determined constructs.

Of this increasingly large segment of Israeli society, Esther Fuchs (2005) observes that

> "[H]aredi women continue to depend on male authorities for instruction and guidance . . . [furthermore] Israeli culture as a whole embodies women; the cultural emphasis on women's corporeal functions transfers discursive and

social control over their bodies to male authorities whereby women's autonomy is undermined and they are literally made physically sick." (11-12)

Just after soiling her hair, Amalia weeps as she walks in a disheveled state through the streets of Jerusalem. Coming upon a group of women she is set upon:

> [T]he women threw me on the raised camp outside the square, my clothes torn, my face filthy . . . the women in kerchiefs [a sign of being religiously observant] turned back . . . shrieking harder in the weeping of lamentation, as if to atone for the time they had wasted taking care of the impure woman [Amalia]. . . . A dense mass of flesh pressed to flesh, flesh of my flesh . . . helpless. Not noticing with their pure faith the destruction that was decreed. (370-371)

These so-called religious women seize upon the distraught Amalia and beat her. All the elements that go into an hysterical mob reaction are here—shrieking, packed flesh, pure faith. To these women, Amalia is a threatening, disruptive force. She is not dressed properly, behaving in ways that violate the codes dictating what is acceptable. Banding together in a malevolent, energetic mass, the group goes after that which dares to differentiate itself. It's a chilling depiction of the brutality of a mob, and it's no comfort that this is a mob of women. Like Amalia, they have internalized male messages of how a religious woman should comport herself in the world, how a woman should walk the streets of Jerusalem. In the novel's denouement, Amalia is literally made dead, the furthest extension of Fuchs' idea of sickness taking over the disenfranchised female body.

Discussion thus far has focused on Amalia in relation to the exterior world that dictates the rules governing her life. There is, however, another Amalia whose interior life is rich in other imaginings. This Amalia is a thinker, a writer, a weaver, an artist. While it is unfortunately true that Amalia comes to be dominated by the judgments of those who destroy her, she also dwells in a space where her own creative impulses reign. Here she pursues self-defined artistic and spiritual truths, expressing them both in words and in the act of weaving. Inside this emotional space lives a more benevolent, less tormented self. Amalia is an expert weaver, as well as one who reacts to the written word with a robust intellectual delight which exhilarates her and us, even as it leads to darkness. It is this Amalia who gives the book much of its force and power.

If she were less compelling as an individual animated by her own sense of spiritual truth, her story would simply be that of a woman destroyed by a cruel, sexist, fundamentalist religious world. While Amalia's suicide is certainly impelled by the twisted visions of that world, it's also a choice based on her own conclusion that this is where her god-quest has taken her. Fearlessness and thoughtful clarity illuminate her self-administered end. Through her creativity, she has envisioned god-as-sexual being, a radically rich notion. Tying together the strands of her journey, she reaches a fulfillment of sorts as she concludes her own self-directed acts of writing and weaving.

This is not an argument for suicide as a desirable way of tying up loose emotional and spiritual ends. It is an attempt to point out that Amalia's search to find a connection with the divine is a convincing one. She constantly evokes traditional Jewish textual sources to explain her existence and to shape her conversations with God. Her passionate love for language never falters. Whether one is a believer or a skeptic or a scoffer, Amalia's unending search for personal truth is affecting. Cutting off her life prematurely demonstrates all too painfully her inability to reconcile her invisibility within text to her fevered yearning for the transcendent. Amalia insists on making herself visible to her text-based God, and suicide is her final attempt to say to that God, "here I am; see me."

Other attempts to be visible to this god on her own terms, specifically through weaving and writing, have failed. The novel itself is her confessional, a record of her love affair all the way to its—and her—literal end. She is also weaving a cloth to cover a synagogue ark in which sacred scrolls are kept. These commitments—to tell her story in both fabric and in words—are central in understanding Amalia as the multilayered woman she is. She is not a cipher lacking a substantial interior life; she is a seeker whose art is integral to her relentless search to connect with what she holds most dear. She fashions a text woven from cloth she makes and from words she chooses. While her text does not ultimately prevail, its very existence is a challenge to the dominant discourse.

Weaving is an oft-used metaphor for describing a particularly female way of ordering experience. Feminist theologian Carol Christ (2001) suggests that

> The image of weaving . . . [names women] . . . as creators of culture . . . as poets. They connect the image of weaving with the Goddess, she who weaves time and fate . . . she who is with us today as we attempt to transform images of the female body and women's power. Through the metaphor of weaving, contemporary women creating a new culture are linked to a heritage of female creativity going back to prehistory. (41)

Amalia is surely weaving "time and fate." Her woven sacred objects are material items which concretize abstract passions embodying felt truths. In making a cloth used to cover the structure wherein the sacred *Torah* (Hebrew Bible) is kept, she's creating an object in which to enfold sacred text. Symbolically, this weaving will clothe her God located in the words of the *Torah*, enshrouding divinity in a woman's handmade fabric.

The scholar Susan Handelman (1982) suggests that "the Rabbinic concept of language and meaning . . . has at its center the concept of the divinity of the text. . . . It [the *Torah*] was written with letters of black fire upon a background of white fire. . . . The material ink and parchment are seen as the garments for the divine wisdom enclothed therein" (37). In other words, text itself is a sacred artifact, a place wherein God dwells. The divine is made manifest through language. Ink and paper are, if you will, clothing for the insights of God. This image is startlingly appropriate to describe Amalia's embodiment of her god as she weaves a garment that will literally cover the divine body of words.

Surely, Amalia's weaving is creating a redefined culture, one that challenges male hegemony. Within Israel, secular Jews make up a majority of the country's population. But they have ceded much power to fundamentalist Jews in ways that are destabilizing. They have permitted extreme elements to hijack the definition of religion. Govrin's character suggests another way that religion might be framed. In Amalia's case, her inability to find a way through the religious thicket is fatal. For in the end Amalia sees the *Torah* along with its cloth covering as her funeral shroud.

Envisioning her death, she views herself "Cloaked in the Torah as in a garment, the parchment scrolls wound around my breast . . . I and the fabric of my life. I and You in one word" (211). In this creative weaving, divine word is made cloth. When the end comes, everything—Amalia, the *Torah* curtain and its text, God—will be one. God and word and corporeal self will be united via this object, erasing boundaries between human and divine. The completed weaving signals the completed life. Amalia's woven cover is a gift of love for the ever present-in-absence beloved God, a sensual act and a key component in the fulfillment of all her desire—culminating in her longing to die and be wedded to God. Her descriptions are sensual, lush details creating a world of sumptuousness even as they point towards the blankness of death. Envisioning dead Amalia wrapped in a *Torah* cloth of her own making is to imagine her fusion with God through an act that distills the yearning to embody her spiritual self.

Along with weaving, writing is the other element of Amalia's artistic fashioning of her soul's journey. As she is the book's narrator, we know at once that words are central to containing her inner spiritual turmoil. It is not until the end of the book—and the imminent end of her life—that she articulates her passion for words. Putting aside her pen as she prepares to kill herself is an almost unbearable act of leave-taking. Having completed preparations for death, only one thing remains: "To finish, to put down the pen" (430). This final act of abnegation is the most profoundly difficult. Struggling to cease her outpouring of words is rendered in exquisite segments as we watch Amalia's agonized disengagement from writing, which along with weaving has given her tortured journey coherence. The poignancy of her connection to language is breathtaking: "And then I ran inside, to write something more before the end. Excitement unravels the breathing . . . The light is coming to an end, and my hand is still reaching to write. . . . As if something is still revealed, clarified for the first time" (432).

When "Everything is ready, I am purified" (433) and Amalia has performed all the rites enabling her to die in a cleansed state, she still cannot stop her writing. "I'm still bent over here at the open window, savoring the new taste of calm. Putting the pen to the sheet of paper with a new ease" (433). In fact, so life-giving and preserving is the act of writing that she envisions a future even as she prepares to shut everything down:

> I'll open them [the pages] in years to come, after everything . . . I'll lean on my thin arm and I'll read, slowly turning the pages, leaning over the writing with dull eyes . . . I will slowly go through the pages, reading what is written with the transparent breathing of someone who has accepted and blessed everything. (433-34)

It's an image of Amalia's life redeemed through language. In this alternative narrative, the woman has created her own text and made sense of existence in her own terms. But it's not enough to offset that reality which has been articulated through the male-determined reading of religious text which Amalia has internalized. This brief visitation of continuity achieved through the healing power of her own words is not enough to stop Amalia's inexorable progress towards making her end come now. We're very close to that end: "The body is silent, wrapped in a distant dizziness . . . The paper and fingers guiding the pen are slipping away" (435).

Amalia's narrative is just about over. To the very last second of life, language is foremost in consciousness along with her desire to be with God. She's leaving her words to be found with her body. Final utterances and the book's concluding sentence are "The remnant of the light on the peak opposite is wiped out. Put down the pen. The Lord gives and the Lord takes away; blessed be the name of the Lord. Sabbath" (438). Her dying words refer to the taking away of the pen—most precious tool of all, that which enables her to create text. Juxtaposing an instrument of writing with the power of God to bestow and retract everything of value, Govrin conjures another stunning image of what Amalia most cherishes—words as they come from her own pen to describe passionate adoration of her precious deity.

This ending scene is majestically sad beyond bearing. Readers may feel as though they are in the room with Amalia, desperate to bring her surcease from unbearable suffering with its self-destructive desire to merge with the sacred through death. "Pick up your pen, Amalia," we shout. "Don't lay it down yet." But she cannot be reached. Too much pain, too many memories, too fierce a longing to move to a unity impossible for the living and unlikely for the dead. For Amalia, the only way to resolve the raging contradictions within herself is to annihilate that ground of being from which these agonies sprang. There is not world enough, nor time, for healing. Bound up in a history marked by the destruction of the Holocaust; living in a world of ultra-Orthodox Judaism which tightens her options and denigrates her very essence; seeking through text and art a way to connect to that which she sees as most unattainable except through death, make her suicide if not inevitable then surely understandable.

This person, this Amalia, helps the reader grapple with one kind of response to an unendurable pain as Amalia's notions of God and text are obliterated by the power of Jerusalem's ultra-Orthodox male religious world. Looking to male-interpreted text for guiding wisdom, she found only a despicable self. Traditional Jewish texts are often blinding in their brilliance, offering stunning insight on innumerable levels. Major problems come when the words are given only to men to interpret. Govrin's remarkable achievement is to bring to life a character for whom the power of text is compelling enough to literally die for. The tragedy is that death was the only option in Amalia's attempt to write herself into a hyper-masculinized story.

GOD THE FATHER, FATHER THE GOD (*SNAPSHOTS*)

Govrin's next novel, *Snapshots*, was published in Hebrew in 2002 and in English translation in 2007. *Snapshots* deepens an exploration of a Jewish feminist perspective manifesting itself in a troubled Israeli universe. It too acquaints readers with a woman destined to die in her quest for fulfillment in a male-defined world. The feminism in *Snapshots* is fairly obvious as the book's main character and its narrator, architect and writer Ilana Tzuriel, articulates everything through a passionately held view that a differentiated female point of view perceives the world in marked contrast to traditional male vantage points. Like Amalia, Ilana insists on participating in a male world as a creative, viable human actor. Unlike Amalia, she strives mightily to change this world rather than buying into its premises. Her vision is to change the maleness of the Israel she inhabits, challenging the male perspective by reinterpreting space (as an architect) and text (as a writer). She too is destroyed, though her end probably comes about accidentally rather than being self-determined. The qualifier "probably" has to do with the character's willfulness, a tempestuous nature that might well use an automobile to end it all.

In *The Name*, it is not until the book's conclusion that we are certain the protagonist/narrator will end her story by taking her own life. On the other hand, we learn immediately in the second paragraph of *Snapshots*, that "Ilana was killed in an accident on the Strasbourg-Munich autobahn" (Govrin 2007, 1). The untimely deaths of these two narrators is somehow not surprising. In both novels, each is pushed over the edge in a struggle against the givens of a male-defined cosmos which leaves little room for them. Amalia battles within the universe of fundamentalist ultra-Orthodox Judaism. Ilana faces obstacles in attempting to express a feminized paradigm in the world of male-dominated architecture as it exists in Jerusalem. For Ilana, traditional male architecture reflects deeply held beliefs about male-female relationships. In addition, it encodes assumptions about how Israelis and Palestinians live—or fail to live—in harmony. Ilana is convinced she can change this out of "completely different notions of place, of dwelling . . . the feminine terminology of temporary, open planning" (73-75).

It is almost a cliché to have Amalia and Ilana's lives come to an early end; in pre-feminist literature, the death of the heroine was a standard punishment for breaking the rules. On the other hand, there would seem to be no possible way for either Amalia or Ilana to resolve the insoluble contradictions of their intense lives. Death becomes their only respite, the ending of journeys that are the opposite of fairy tales. Given the intense all-or-nothing nature of each protagonist, death is one of the few options offering resolution and surcease from great psychic pain. Without arguing the merits or demerits of such a denouement, it makes a kind of sense in these contexts. Neither of these women can find a viable way to live in the Israeli world they inhabit.

We get the news of Ilana's death from a woman named Tir-sa, a childhood friend of hers. Alain, Ilana's husband, has telephoned Tir-sa with the news and asked her to come and collect Ilana's personal papers from him. In making this request, Alain tells Tir-sa, "Personal notes . . . were in her handbag . . . everything in Hebrew. It will take me years to decipher. You know, our personal abyss " (1). Ilana's marriage is troubled, with she and her husband living in an ongoing state of emotional detachment. Her now widowed husband cannot decipher his wife's written text—as he could not read her when she was alive—and he must give the words to a woman for explication.

This less than ideal, distant marriage is only one of Ilana's many complicated relationships with a number of different men. *Snapshots* is a record of a series of entanglements she has had or continues to have with Sayyid, a Palestinian artist and theater director; with her husband Alain; with her Israeli cousin David; with Belgian Claude whose life is devoted to promoting socially conscious architecture—among others. For Ilana, sexual relationships with a variety of men are central to her existence. At one point, she writes that "a gathering of . . . [her] cohort of lovers . . . came like a group of guardian angels " (115). Her many lovers are like childhood literature's good fairies watching over her. Sexual connections are how Ilana orders her universe, using her body to hold together the often conflicting worlds represented by the men with whom she is involved. As with Amalia, Ilana's body is her primary means of reconciling intense inner contradictions. Ilana gets a great deal more enjoyment from her sexuality than does Amalia. But like the distraught Amalia, Ilana looks to sexuality to make whole that which is fragmented.

There is little to no interaction between Ilana and other women throughout the tale. Even Tir-sa, who introduces the narrative, disappears after page six. It's a telling disappearance, placing Amalia in a world defined primarily by men. Except for this beginning, the entire book consists of the deceased Ilana speaking to us through her diary, made available courtesy of her [absent] friend's devoted efforts. The minor role of Tir-sa in the book's structure is a reflection of Ilana's preoccupation with men as those whom she will conquer by means of her body as well as her intellect. She is no shrinking violet, nor is she a woman who doubts her body's appeal to males. The book is sprinkled with comments reflecting a woman (unlike Amalia) who views herself as someone physically desirable, never losing sight of her sexuality as a potential for connection. Describing herself in a slightly coy approving tone, Ilana writes, "I in the black leather jacket, my face peeping out of the red scarf . . . thrusting into its edges the disheveled curls, lighting up the face . . . [a] face . . . completely covered by the mane, a kind of curly-haired Gorgon . . . above tight jeans" (45-46). The important point is that like Amalia, who internalizes a male-defined world, Ilana does the same in her relentless use of her body to gain entry into places she wishes to enter but will never fully inhabit.

The relevance to this character in shedding light on Israeli culture stems initially from the struggles she wages as a fiercely independent, self-assured woman committed to making her mark as an architect whose work contributes to ending conflict between Jews and Palestinians. She is engaged in designing a structure which will serve as a monument to peace in the tormented Middle East. In a hilltop in Jerusalem, she aims to erect a "'Settlement of Huts,' and individuals or groups will come to it. They'll build their Huts, and they'll live in them for seven days. People can come from all over the world, without visas, without a police check, it will be an open area . . . in the heart of Jerusalem" (107).

This notion of a temporary dwelling place is taken from a ritual observed during the Jewish holiday of *Sukkot* when observant Jews spend a week living in temporary shelters erected in their backyards. The temporary nature of these structures is an essential element in their design and use. Ilana interprets the transitional mode of living in these nonpermanent shelters as a quintessentially female way of structuring space and writes that "Returning to my studio . . . and sketching until dawn. . . . The hand bringing the infant to the breast, walking from the bed to cooking, to reading, filling out this kernel that nourishes the space. What turned into my personal style, called 'neo-humane architecture,' 'the female, organic architecture of Tsuriel [her last name]" (41). Furthermore, she insists that this feminized architecture has larger implications: "I'm at a stage of opening a new reality, with dimensions of letting go of the hold on this blood-soaked place. I want to show that the place par excellence of envy ownership can exist beyond the hold of human beings" (172). "This is my interpretation, in feminine architecture, of Sabbatical, letting go of the flow of Deliverance. Not the waters of the Prophet's rage, but an eternal flow . . . this living womb of Jerusalem" (187).

Ilana is working to structure a space in the midst of tormented Jerusalem which embodies the idea that only by letting go can something meaningful be realized. As with Amalia's weaving, she seeks to embody her ideas materially; in this case, she will express an original paradigm through designing new architectural structures. And like Amalia, Ilana bases her rationale on traditional textual sources. She is less tormented by notions of God as expressed in text than is Amalia, but text does play a central role in her thinking. Similar to Amalia, Ilana is profoundly shaped by traditional Jewish notions from biblical and other ancient sources. And she is deeply influenced by her Zionist father's textual writings. In addition, her architectural work is in Jerusalem, where male minions of fundamentalist Judaism exercise enormous power through a strict and often narrow interpretation of text. The fervent, doctrinaire, male religiosity of Jerusalem is the backdrop for Ilana's journey as it is for Amalia's.

Ilana articulates the *raison d'etre* for her Israeli architecture in response to what she sees as male-determined spatial concepts. Whereas Amalia works primarily with permutations of time, Ilana's engagements are with space and its possibilities for transcendent meaning. Her vision of space, she insists, promulgates the idea that the land of Israel belongs to no one and to everyone. To put it mildly, this is a radical idea, challenging the core assumption that Jerusalem and Israel belong only to the Jews. Ilana is passionate in her belief, and she is adamant that it is a uniquely feminine worldview: "Think about a place that can't be owned! Especially the Land of Israel, Jerusalem, the place everybody wants to conquer, to own! Jerusalem, the longed-for city, the woman, the place of yearning . . . to let go of her" (74).

Ilana employs female images repeatedly, particularly in reference to the allure of Jerusalem, near-mythic city in Israel the land and Israel the symbol. An icon in stories that shape the Jewish mythos, Jerusalem's stature as the jewel in the Jewish crown remains undiminished—with often disastrous results. Anat Hoffman (2011), Executive Director of the Israel Religious Action Center and Director of Women of the Wall comments "Jerusalem is a harsh city to live in. It is a city in struggle, a struggle between narrow-minded Judaism and pluralistic Judaism, a battle for appropriate representation for all city inhabitants."

In Govrin's two novels, Jerusalem is a site where fundamentalist Jewish enclaves flourish and exert unrelenting destructive pressure in defining how Jews are supposed to live. In seeking to free up "the place everybody wants to conquer," Ilana continually likens Jerusalem to a bound-up woman. She juxtaposes conflicting aspects of female experience in such descriptions of Jerusalem as, "Object of desire of God, prophets, believers . . . Jerusalem the woman. Loyal, unfaithful, saint and whore, the city of God's lust, the city that maddens all those who yearn to own her, to demand an exclusive claim to her " (114).

This description of Jerusalem applies to Ilana herself. Her sexuality is a thread which both links her to others and also threatens to destroy her and any person who would claim her. *The Name*'s Amalia comes to see Jerusalem, particularly the dirt of its earth, as darkly punishing. Ilana sees a brazen and alive place, one continually eluding any attempt at outside control. Her Jerusalem is alive with possibilities, with she herself as an active player in determining its future. Her own identity, like Jerusalem's, is reflected in the contradictions inherent in the clichéd but apt opposing notions of saint and whore.

This Jerusalem-in-Ilana is contained in her unshakable conviction that as a powerfully sensual, sexual and creative woman, she can change the world through her work. And she will be aided in this undertaking by her attractive body. Her architecture will transform troubled spaces into places of peaceful cohabitation; her body will maintain the relationships needed to make this happen. Ilana's passion to build an architectural monument, one that is a female paradigm of space enabling connection between Israelis and Palestinians, is unrelenting. Her claims for its efficacy are untinged by self-doubt. Screaming at her husband, she tells him "I build . . . huts in the heart of war. Just to believe, Alain. Understand that. Without that belief I can't live. . . . That's my life " (210).

Like Amalia, Ilana *embodies* those things which most matter. Architectural work is indispensable to that embodiment, as is intense sexuality in which physical relationships order the universe. Beyond her professional role, and more than a wife, more than a mother—both of which she is—sexuality is crucial to comprehending Ilana. With her two young sons, she is a loving and open parent, physically reassuring. As a lover, she revels in her body and takes uninhibited pleasure in sexual intercourse. With Palestinian lover Say yid, there is "the gushing evoked in me again . . . flowing forth in a thick, deep flow . . . the rage of limbs, the hasty sucking . . . subsiding breaths" (284-285). She and her estranged husband Alain retain a powerful physical connection, and even after a long separation there is "the groping. Like going down old paths" (293).

Interacting with the men in her life, Ilana's body is the means to unify their histories and hold together disparate narratives. Physicality makes it possible to somehow contain conflicting and yet interlocking Israeli stories: her lover Sayyid's Palestinian story, her husband Alain's Holocaust history, and her father's narrative as part of the story of Israel's early settlers. As the book's narrator, we see all the men through her gaze and learn about them only what she chooses to tell. The men are screens upon whom she projects her own and her country's history. Absorbing the various skeins of the Zionist story, Ilana seeks to shape a rewritten conclusion. Ultimately Ilana's body is a kind of text upon which she will both write her own life and create a different Israeli national narrative.

But Ilana herself is Israeli, and in telling her version of the story she does not fully include Other. Sayyid's story fades into insignificance. We get a little of Sayyid's history as a displaced Israeli Palestinian. But he is not a fully fleshed out character whom we get to know in depth. His tale of life as a Palestinian artist—though he insists his story's time has come—remains skeletal. He helps fill in the blanks on the Palestinian side of the ledger, but his role is largely as a foil for Ilana's torments. Ultimately, she sees him as unwilling to let go of an atavistic hold on the land. Therefore, he is seen as part of the problem in making Israel truly free for all. Their narratives diverge, and Ilana writes "we're cut off, each one engulfed in his own story" (252). As Sayyid disappears from view she tells us, "The contact with Sayyid has sunk under the skin. . . . We haven't talked since I've returned. He hasn't called and I haven't gotten in touch either" (296).

Like Sayyid on the Palestinian side, her Holocaust survivor mate Alain represents another major element in the meta-history of the Jews. And as with her lover, we get only a sketchy, clichéd view of her husband. Ilana tells us that, "When they [the Nazis] took them . . . [Alain] was six years old. His mother urged him to run . . . he hid behind the garbage bins . . . something in Alain . . . always remains a withdrawn child" (37-8). Alain works to discover long-hidden Jewish archives, to document Jewish loss and displacement. Fundamentally he does not believe that Israel is a safe nation. Enraged at both his wife's liberalism and the futility of an Israeli homeland, he makes his wrath clear: "The Zionist lunacy of gathering all the Jews in one place, preparing the conditions for an easy final extermination! . . . How come you leftists don't understand that everything is part of a long-range plan to destroy the Jewish people" (41-42). Like Sayyid, Alain too is a kind of caricature existing only as a platform upon which Ilana acts out her own drama. He represents the tormented, avenging Jew who has lost everything to the Holocaust and spends his life seeking some kind of revenge for this catastrophe.

Most significantly, at times for Ilana, "Alain and Sayyid changed in me, got mixed up in one another" (48). She experiences these two archetypal figures—the creative, vibrant, artistic Palestinian and the driven, scholarly, haunted Jew—merging inside of her. Within her are embodied two of the major strands of the Jewish Israeli narrative, and she cannot always tell where one stops and the other begins.

And then, near the story's end, we learn that Ilana is pregnant. The baby might be Sayyid's or it might be her husband Alain's: "The test was positive. . . . Allowing myself to be with Sayyid, and with Alain, even though I had stopped taking the pill . . . I'm pregnant" (298). The question as to who is actually the nascent baby's father encapsulates this merging of narratives and the confusion Ilana lives out. This fetus might be the beginning of a child of a Palestinian or the child of the Holocaust's Alain, a harbinger of the future or a harking back to the past. Ilana is literally embodying the future, and her uncertainty regarding paternity is a crowning metaphor for all the claims and counter-claims as to who is entitled to that body called Israel.

If we consider that for a woman, body experiences are essential to self-identity and to being grounded in the world, Ilana can be understood in terms of her own body as the alpha and omega of all that she does. Early on she states, "the body always conducted its own story" (41). In the next to the last sentence written in her diary before her death in a car crash, she reiterates this: "The body speaks in its own language" (302). Shortly after she express-es this thought comes the end—of her body, of her baby, of her holding together the contradictions that are Sayyid and Alain, of the oppositions that are Israel today.

In her embodiment of contradictions, Ilana is a fervid lover to both her illicit Palestinian paramour and to her Jewish husband. But important as Sayyid and Alain are in attempts to contain clashing worlds, her real lover and the person most fully realized in her imagination is Ilana's deceased father. It would be illuminating to engage in any number of psychoanalytical-ly based interpretations of their relationship. However, for our purposes, this father/daughter enmeshment will be examined chiefly to illuminate the cen-trality of founding Zionist text to contemporary Israelis like Ilana. A variety of secular texts set out the parameters for what the new state should be, and these founding writings still remain a determinant of Israeli national con-struction.

Ilana addresses all narrative discourse to her deceased father. To her, he embodies the founding Zionist dream and represents the invaluable visions of Israel's pioneer settlers. The first words in her diary are "Dear father, once again with you" (12). She sees her story as bound up with his, asking him "How to hold the fragments of our torn story" (15). Writing of her architectu-ral dreams, she says, "[this project] is dedicated to him. He's with me all the time I plan. . . . I think about him, about his dream" (75). As Amalia wrote everything down in an attempt to explain herself to God, so Ilana's diary is an ongoing conversation with her father. She and her father are connected through text—via his writings which she obsessively peruses as well as her diary addresses to him. Going through papers after his death, she quotes from the first page of his notebook and opens a window into her father's world:

> In these pages, I will write down events from my childhood in the small town,
> and from the fifty years of my life and work in Israel. Those chapters in a long
> route with one common denominator. Love of Israel, yearnings for Israel and

building Israel. In all of us . . . there exists a profound and lofty sense, the great privilege we have earned: the establishment of a homeland for the Hebrew people. (248-49)

On the title page her father has written "To the memory of my parents, my brother, and my sister, who remained in the town, and were killed in the slaughter of European Jewry" (249).

There, in all its clarity, is a central foundation story of the Zionist undertaking. Anyone who would even begin to understand contemporary Israeli thinking must understand how profoundly this loss and displacement narrative informs the current Israeli master narrative. For Ilana, her father's story is inextricably linked to the story of the birth of Israel; no distinction comes between his individual history and the national narrative. Ilana reads her father's story as aligned with her own dream of an Israel for all people, and she conjures a man of compassionate largeness of view. Her reverence for her father's text is manifest in her insistence on mining his papers for all they might reveal both about his particular history and about the founding of the state. Ilana takes from his text the basis for her own attachment to the land. Most significantly, Ilana begins to see her story and her father's as one and the same. The boundaries between them dissolve: "And your voice rising in me all this year. Impregnates me with your story, our story, without any difference anymore, Father" (250).

Themes in Govrin's two novels explicitly link here, primarily the attachment to a beloved divine expressed via language. To Ilana, her father is a god and his text is holy. Her father's writings expressing his visions of Israel have the weight of sacred scripture. And like much sacred scripture, they are remnants of an earlier, purer time of untarnished possibilities. Her yearning for him, expressed in vivid sexual terms, is a desire to fuse with this god-like being beyond earthly reach. Sexual longings are an expression of joining her fate with that of her father's and with the land he loved. And this love is based on a so-called sacred story, the Zionist narrative of the Jews articulating their right to the land of Israel.

Like Amalia wrapping herself in the holy words of the *Torah* curtain, Ilana joins her narrative with her father's. From this merging of their stories, her impregnation by her father via words, it is only a small step to her fantasies of her father as her most desired lover. Amalia's beloved God-the-father is Ilana's beloved father-the-god.

Here is Ilana describing a dream about and to her father:

I lie without moving . . . so that whoever is lying next to me won't notice that you're standing there. And only, in silence, drinking in the sight of you close by, taking the blanket off me, running your eyes over my naked body. And then, carefully, lying down next to me. . . . Body along body. Enormous excitement. (291)

Earlier, she writes of finding

> nude photos of you [her father] . . . Standing on a rock . . . the light flooding
> the shining skin of your erect, muscular body. . . . I'd stand in the street,
> looking at you, amazed at the beating of my heart, at my bursting joy. . . . And
> the dreams of making love with you . . . you're suspended above me, slowly
> descending to me. . . . Mouth to mouth and groin to groin. (31- 32)

Ilana's final unambiguously sexual image of her father comes just before she
is killed when she writes, "until the genetic test, fantasizing that you're the
father of the child. That your seed has impregnated the Hut of my womb"
(300). You can't find too many metaphors as explicit as that for describing an
intense desire to fuse with your father-god and bring forth a child from that
union. Ilana's desire to consummate this relationship is a longing to meld her
story with her father's story, to be part of an idealized version of Israel by
entangling with one who contributed to the Zionist *ur*-text. It's the same
yearning which impelled Amalia's wish to fuse with God. She, too, wanted
to be part of the creation story and to seamlessly blend her narrative with the
maker of the narrative—God. These women are not mad. Rather they are
seekers after their own truths, willing to go wherever the search may lead.
They cry out: let me be part of a grand and glorious story; let my body be
used in the service of connecting that which is broken apart; let me be a
vehicle for sacred text.

For both women, foundational Jewish texts are fundamental in shaping
their lives. Each of them wants to merge with the creators of these guiding
texts. For Amalia, that is God, and for Ilana, it's her father. That the master
authors are male authority figures does not mean these two women are not
worthy of respect from a feminist perspective. Their journeys illustrate how
deeply ingrained are age-old notions of what is most desirable, most worth
living and dying for. That these male authorities are impossible to access—
God is notoriously hard to locate and Ilana's father is deceased—adds to the
maddening elusiveness of what these two women are after.

Futile as their search is, it is fundamentally subversive and life-affirming
as they strive to embody their gods. Neither Ilana nor Amalia personally
triumphs in the end; both die young without having reconciled achingly
contradictory feelings. But we have come to contextualize the centrality of a
father-like God and a god-like father as objects of sexual desire who are part
of a nation's sacred story as understood by women. The significance of
feminine sexuality in matters of Israeli cultural identity is to focus attention
on permutations that can result when human beings take seriously a transcendent creator and engage themselves in dialogue with such a being/metaphor.
When the human beings are two passionate women, we come to a new
understanding of how God and text may meet in a woman's body. What

comes out of this encounter may yet shift the way we read the sacred narratives woven into contemporary Israeli life. Amalia and Ilana are authors of a more inclusive national narrative wrenched from the depths of their innermost, conflicted selves.

NOTES

1. Bronner, Ethan and Isabel Kershner. (2012). "At a time when there is no progress on the Palestinian dispute, Israelis are turning inward and discovering that an issue they had neglected—the place of the ultra-Orthodox Jews—has erupted into a crisis. And it is centered on women. . . . Moshe Halbertal, a professor of Jewish philosophy at Hebrew University [said] "This is an immense ideological and moral challenge that touches at the core of life . . . it is the main issue that the rabbis are losing sleep over."

2. Rosenberg, Oz. (2012). "A woman was attacked in her car by ultra-Orthodox extremists—the latest in a series of incidents apparently sparked by what members of the town's Haredi community view as immodest dress. A crowd of ultra-Orthodox men jumped on [the] 27-year-old['s] . . . car in the Haredi . . . neighborhood. . . . Members of the crowd smashed her car windows and punctured her four tires before spilling bleach on the inside of her car . . . [and] she believed the men were going to set her on fire. The incident follows the highly publicized case of [an] 8-year-old [girl] . . . who was reportedly spat at for her supposedly insufficiently modest dress despite the fact that she comes from a religious family."

3. *Haredi* is often translated as "trembling before God"; a more literal meaning is "fearful" or "anxious". *Haredim* is the plural form.

4. According to Israel's Central Bureau of Statistics "the ultra-Orthodox population will number 1.1 million people by 2019, compared with 750,000 in 2009. By 2059, there will be anywhere between 2.73 million and 5.84 million haredim—a 264%-686% increase." Reported inwww.ynetnews.com/articles/0,7340,L-4209333,00.html.

Chapter Four

The Demise of the New Jew

Zeruya Shalev

> How fine
> you are, my love,
> my perfect one
> (Song of Songs, 15)

Early Zionism conjured a vision of the emancipated Jew striding over his regained homeland, a reinvigorated—male—Jewish body dominating a newly liberated Jewish land. Zionist narratives highlight the masculine hero. The role and status of women is far less heroic, articulated mainly in relation to the new Israeli man positioned at the center of this reconfigured world. Today's Israeli lives in a world far different from that envisioned by early Zionism, but the ideals set forth at the State's founding continue to influence communal self-perception. Particularly in the nation's beginnings but still today, Zionism was the "dominant language through which Israelis . . . rendered meaningful their collective history and identity" (Silberstein 1999, 5). In what some describe as a post-Zionist age, such maps of meaning are no longer adequate. Today's Zion is not the promising world of the pioneer settlers. But outdated as these old maps are, they continue to hold sway over the discourse and behavior of contemporary Israelis.

This is not unusual. The origin myths of nations tend to remain influential, long after a country has moved beyond its youth and entered middle age or beyond. Changed as the United States is from the early days of the republic, rhetoric constantly references the past. Citizens of the United States, like citizens in Israel, hearken back to the good old days. Israel's good old days began with a dream of repossessing the land. This resettlement would give rise to generations of Jews whose lives would unfold into a new openness.

The new Jew would be liberated—politically, socially, physically, sexually. The land would yield milk and honey. Persecution, destruction and fear for survival would no longer dominate as the new Jew tilled the land and honed the ability to defend what was his.

Zionist writings posited that relationships between men and women were bound up in notions of what the new Jewish state should be, as well as what the new Jewish male would be. A sexually healthy Judaism was to be part of the new Hebrew man and his mate, relations freed from the debilitation of life inside the suffocating social frameworks of Europe. Eros as a component of early Zionist imaginings assumed that Jews would remake themselves in the embrace of a desired and desiring land. Eros, while not totally unbound, would be at greater liberty to reinvigorate Jewish life and its domestic institutions. A profound connection existed between pioneer Israeli Jews' desire to free themselves from oppressive political nets and how life in erotic, sexual spheres was envisioned. As David Biale (1992) puts it, "The individual body became a microcosm for the national body politic. To create a new image of the Jewish body became a symbol for creating a new Jewish nation" (178). "The ideology of erotic liberation was always a means to realize the broader nationalist goals of Zionism" (192).

Zeruya Shalev illuminates ties between the body physical and the body politic, exploring dis-ease in individuals struggling in a post-Zionist world. Shalev's novels, *Love Life* and *Husband and Wife*, pose a counter-narrative to the hoped for versions of what it would mean to be a liberated man and woman in contemporary Israel. Implicit in her work is a critique of assumptions in Zionist discourse relating to matters of sexuality and gender. Shalev's characters embody both nostalgia for the past and ambivalence about its covert messages. In her universe, domestic turmoil undercuts expectations pertaining to private life encoded in the nation's origin stories. Her works challenge the gendered ideals of masculine/feminine as set forth at the nation's beginning, a time when "Zionism appropriated the negative image of the male Jew and transformed it into the positive image of the 'new Jew' or the 'muscle Jew' . . . [creating] a virile new Hebrew man, an ideal that shaped the emerging culture of modern Israel" (Hoffman 2007, 36-37).

The men in Shalev's books are impotent, confused, sterile, suffering from hysterical paralysis. Their unhappiness is reflected in their marriages and affairs, and these domestic vignettes frame larger societal issues. Her women grapple with contradictory notions of what it means to be a wife, mother, lover, worker. Zionism is a phallocentric framework, and women's roles are chiefly defined in traditional ways. Shalev's women seek to free themselves from strictures which have their genesis in the world according to men. It is a difficult battle and one they often lose.

Aside from eroticism between individuals, desire was linked to feelings for the land as an object of longing. Early on, material Israel was sometimes seen as a beckoning lover. An intriguing new book, *Land and Desire in Early Zionism*, argues for the impossibility of understanding the passion of Zionism unless one comprehends its profound roots in an erotic attachment to the soil of Israel. "The pioneers themselves," argues Boaz Neumann (2011), ". . . justified their enterprise in various political, economic, ideological, and historical-religious terms . . . But the one recurring motif is *desire* for the land of Israel. The world . . . of the [pioneers is] saturated with articulation of attraction, craving, pining, and love for the Land" (7). Shalev's characters have sex with one another, but underlying their couplings and de-couplings is an erotic connection to the land itself, either directly or through means of a warrior hero guide or via an attempt to reconnect with older, "authentic" Zionist heroes. Eros and its complications inform Shalev's work, some of its roots traceable to founding nationalist visions of men and women. But early expectations are no longer viable containers for the ongoing state of unease characterizing Israel today. The breakdowns of the inhabitants in Shalev's intimate domestic worlds reflect the demise of a coherent framework which once made sense of it all.

LOVE IN A TIME OF WOE (*LOVE LIFE*)

Shalev (1997), herself a woman, writes tales told by women in a time of malaise. *Love Life* is narrated by Ya'ara, the twenty-eight-year-old daughter of Shlomo and Rachel Korman, wife of Yoni, and lover to Aryeh. She is also a university graduate student, seen as having a great deal of potential. In the first scene, on arriving at her parents' apartment, Ya'ara is confronted with an unknown male guest who opens their door. Startled, she says, "He was not my father and not my mother so why did he open the door of their house to me, filling the narrow space with his body . . . and in a weak voice I asked, what's happened to my parents" (1).

Her querulous tone is that of someone feeling displaced, confused by a situation markedly different from what was anticipated. The skewed encounter occurs in a locale to which Ya'ara is intimately connected, her parents' dwelling where she herself lived for a time. A familiar past is thrown off by an unexpected present. Things are not what they are supposed to be.

The man blocking the door, Aryeh Even, is her parents' childhood friend. The answer to Ya'ara's puzzled inquiry directed to Aryeh—"what's happened to my parents"—will unfold as readers learn about her parents' links to this old friend. The lives of all of these people are deeply intertwined; what happened between them in the past has shaped present realities. Just as significantly, the daughter's extended sexual encounter with Aryeh will profoundly influence future family circumstances. Calling their liaison a love affair would be inaccurate. As their coupling proceeds, love is the most

elusive element in what takes place between Ya'ara and Aryeh. Neediness on
both sides predominates.

Immediately following Ya'ara's query, she relates the scene that follows:
"[Aryeh] opened his big, gray mouth . . . my name fluttered in his mouth like
a fish in a net. . . . I crossed the empty living room, and opened the closed
door of their bedroom" (1). In this first encounter, Ya'ara is figuratively
entrapped by Aryeh, prey enmeshed in his web. Furthermore, the house's
living room is an empty space, and the bedroom is closed off. In essence,
neither lively nor erotic spaces exist in this house. Along with spatial dead-
ends, references to human and animal body parts recur throughout the narrative. The persistence of animal images suggests another level of Eros: its
instinctual and a-rational aspects. The narrator's name, Ya'ara, means "for-
est" and Aryeh's surname, Even, means "stone." Such names resonate with
allusions to natural spaces, to the world of the erotic, of forests, animals and
bodies in the night.

Aryeh's body as it interacts with Ya'ara's frames the novel's events.
Aryeh, in his sixties, and Ya'ara, thirty years old, encapsulate generational
differences. In addition, their interactions allude to the persistent shadow
presence of early Zionism as Ya'ara seeks to connect herself to persons who
embody aspects of the country's founding narratives. As the novel begins,
male Aryeh's body is filling up the narrow opening leading to Ya'ara's
parental home. He occupies, if you will, the narrow birth canal of her origins.
Later he will colonize her own intimate narrow opening. She is certainly no
child at thirty years old, but Ya'ara's search for meaningful connections to an
adult world is hampered. Her symbolic birth and consequent emergence into
autonomous adulthood are impeded by Aryeh's looming presence.

Entering her parents' bedroom, Ya'ara encounters her mother lying in bed
with her father impatiently ministering to her. The long-standing nature of
their relationship with the stranger emerges when her father says, "that's my
friend Aryeh Even, don't you remember Aryeh?", and her mother comments,
"why should she remember him, she wasn't even born when he left the
country" (2). When her father expresses concerns about his guest's discomfort, Ya'ara comments, "He seems to be doing OK . . . he acts as if the place
belongs to him" (2). Aryeh has returned with a strong sense of entitlement to
occupy a central space in their lives. Yes, the place does belong to him—and
so will Ya'ara, though just a baby when he was in his prime.

These three old comrades go back to earlier times in Israel, their age and
status marking them as the antecedents out of which this modern, conflicted
young woman was formed. Ya'ara romanticizes their past, and her nostalgia
for bygone days cripples her ability to grapple with the era in which she lives.
Aryeh chose to leave the country, living most of his life in France. His return
has to do with his wife's ill health. Ya'ara's father left medical studies to
work in a research laboratory. Her mother abandoned herself to bitterness

following the early death of Ya'ara's only sibling. While not at the end of their lives, these three figures are in their sixties. Their preoccupations are not those of the younger woman. Rather they are part of the "good old days," though each has gotten sidetracked from original goals. Wandering off earlier paths, all three have lost the sense of purpose which animated their younger selves.

The inheritor of their shared legacies, Ya'ara, is confused and unhappy. Nothing in her life is going well. Her marriage was undertaken without much thought following a one-night stand with someone other than her now husband. The union is joyless and unfulfilling. In her work life, Ya'ara is consistently late or absent from key meetings at the university, and in danger of losing her chance for an academic appointment. Her relationship with her parents takes up a great deal of psychic space, as she repeatedly visits or engages in interior dialogue with them. The future looms as a source of fear. This new Israeli woman is not doing well. She clings to the past, is miserable in the present, and terrified of the future.

Her fearful uncertainty is such that Ya'ara is in a state of arrested development that manifests in ways great and small. Consider her inability to enjoy flowers:

> I've always been depressed by flowers when they wilt, drooping their dry heads to the jar with its foul-smelling water . . . the beauty isn't worth the ugliness . . . before I remember to throw them out another week will pass. . . . I won't understand where the stink is coming from . . . it will take me such a long time to get over it, the trauma of having a bunch of flowers in the house. (170)

"The beauty isn't worth the ugliness" sums up her paralyzed inability to make a commitment, take a chance. Ya'ara's emphasis is on death over life. It's pain she anticipates, the ache of irretrievable loss. With no faith in the future or its possibilities, she takes comfort in assurances of disaster while at the same time seeking to avoid the inevitable decay that accompanies bloom. This sense of futility is clear when Ya'ara describes her attraction to hospitals: "The familiar hospital smell, medicines and airlessness . . . enveloped me like an old coat, repellent but reassuring, soporific and consoling, redolent of care that was well intended even if it didn't do any good, and it was pleasant to be surrounded by those good intentions, far more pleasant than the cold corridors of the university" (99).

Rejecting the university where she is a student, she retreats from a place of too much vitality, too many destabilizing ideas. The cocooned enclosure of a site for the sick calls to her. In a hospital, Ya'ara feels safe from perplexing challenges. A hospital, unpleasant as it may be, is a place to avoid engaging with the vexing external world. Everything is inverted; places of decay hold more appeal than sites teeming with colorful possibility. As the trauma of dead flowers makes it impossible to enjoy their momentary beauty, so does the heady foment of the university make it a danger zone.

Most significantly, Ya'ara's marriage to Yoni is a microcosm demonstrating all that is wrong in this young woman's erotic world—and by extension, her larger universe. Describing her husband, she says: "There was something missing there, and it took me some time to realize that it was his nose . . . it was small and snub like a baby, a kind of button nose, perfect for a baby but a little absurd on a man" (107).

Her husband's nose is in marked contrast to her own which is "This precious feature, the one I most liked to look at . . . straight and narrow like my mother's " (121). The nose is often used as a stand-in for the male sexual organ, and it is clear that Ya'ara's is bigger than her spouse's. Furthermore, Ya'ara's focus on this part of her husband's anatomy resonates with centuries-old ways in which this facial element has indicated inferiority as non-Jews found ways to revile Jews. As Sander Gilman (1991) has argued, "The specific shape of the Jew's nose indicated the damaged nature, the shortened form, of his penis . . . and this . . . was made a pathological sign [of anti-Semitism]" (189). How ironic that this Israeli woman mocks her husband unconsciously using vocabulary of long-standing anti-Semitic body images.

But Ya'ara's distaste for her husband's nose is just the beginning of a catalogue of ways in which his body is inferior. Along with his babyish appendage of a nose, Yoni's body is a repository of repugnant features, "soft thighs, broad hips, and between the thighs sparse black pubic hair, flabby testicles, and a pink, slightly lopsided penis, and then . . . a drooping little paunch, pale chest, and slightly sagging shoulders" (156). In the end, this woman has no use for this male body. It becomes void, infantile, disposable. As she puts it, "I had always felt more comfortable with [Yoni's] face than with his body, and afterward I lay beside him and we held hands and laced our fingers, naked but sexless, like children . . . indifferent to each other's nudity" (73). No erotic charge animates these two, and Yoni remains a pathetic, lost soul as his wife goes about the business of finding some way to mitigate her emptiness.

When they do have sex, Ya'ara is miserably distant: "my whole body shut down, but he didn't stop . . . intrusive and annoying . . . I almost shook him off rudely but then I said to myself, what do you care" (158). The nullification of Yoni's physicality and of any shared intimacy reveals the fragility of their bond. Her description again harks back to centuries-old canards which held that a Jew's body was a thing to be ignored at best or destroyed at worst. Ya'ara's contempt for her husband's physicality once more mirrors classic anti-Jewish scorn.

The participants in this marriage regress to an earlier, younger time when there was no pressure to behave as mature adults. Washing herself after intercourse, Ya'ara "stood there and looked at him with pity and terror, like looking at a sick baby in its sleep" (159). Earlier, she notes, "We were so lost, the pair of us, orphaned twins . . . sheep that had lost their flock, and all the time I would wonder how to get connected to the right life again" (108). United in the fantasy of a childlike innocence devoid of sexuality, actual sex is perfunctory for Yoni and unpleasant for Ya'ara. Her relationship to him is that of a mother to a (sick) baby as she strokes his hair to urge him into sleep. When not his mother or his sexless comrade, Ya'ara is as a sister: "it turned out we had been born exactly on the same day of the same month, in other words, we were twins" (107) and "had become . . . brother and sister" (38). Few routes to connection exist; only sisterliness obtains, with a tiny hint of calming nurse.

Both psychologically and physically, Yoni is very far from the New Jewish Man of Zionist myth. He lacks any forcefulness, and Ya'ara says of her husband "[When] we began to go out into the world . . . I started hating Yoni . . . the more he loved me the more I hated him . . . his yes was so light, so disappointing, as if he had said no" (107-8). His "yes" so close to his "no" is as flabby as his testicles. In her marital misery, Ya'ara is desperately aware of having lost the life she should be leading—regardless of the fact that any sense of a rightful life remains elusive. The microcosm of the world that is their marriage reflects a set of assumptions gone awry. The ineffectual, weak Yoni and his scornful wife are not strong, happy Hebrew citizens at home in their Zionist garden. They are lost souls, with Ya'ara seeking a new Eden by taking up with a man at least twice her age who offers a return to the certitude of an earlier time.

Ya'ara's most passionate desire is to escape from her stunted baby-man husband: "I felt a hard kicking inside me, as if I had a wild horse in my stomach . . . and it grew stronger and stronger, as if I had a whole stable of wild horses inside me . . . so I got up . . . and then I dragged the suitcase into the living room" (159). A satisfactory adult life remains outside of her experience, a state yet to be discovered. She finds neither meaning nor connection in her marriage; nor is there a sense that being a mother would redeem her. What kicks in her stomach are horses, not babies. Abandoning marriage thrusts Ya'ara into further uncertainty as to who she is and what role she will play as an Israeli woman approaching thirty years old. Bound in a state of arrested development, Ya'ara is frozen.

In addition to arrested development with her husband, there are core issues with her parents. Filling a very large space, another obstacle to emotional maturity lies in Ya'ara's inappropriate ties to them. Continually measuring herself against their expectations, Ya'ara remains a child finding no break from a past that strangles. What happens when younger generations find guiding ideals envisioned by their ancestors hollow? Ya'ara seeks to deflect this question by holding still more tightly to her mother and father and, by extension, to a lover who is part of their generation. She is unwilling and unable to grapple with the challenges inherent in her personal and communal world.

At the very beginning of the narrative, Ya'ara's first question "what's happened to my parents " (1) defined the stranger in the doorway in relation to them when she remarks "He was not my father and not my mother" (1). Preoccupation with her parents often surfaces in romanticized memories of childhood: "suddenly I felt muffled longings for my parents, because whenever the electricity failed the three of us would reluctantly unite, sitting obediently around a single candle. . . . I would look at us and think that we were what's called a given, the kind of thing that can't be changed, a present that was already a past" (109-10). This given is the nuclear family where everything is frozen into an immutable, already-dead present. The desire of Ya'ara to once again sit in a half-lit space with her mother and father is a poignant image of the past as shadowy retreat from a present too brightly lit for this young woman's nerves.

Desire for early childhood comfort continues at a funeral where, "like a good little girl I stood between my mother and my father" (138). Hidden away in her lover's bedroom overhearing her parents' voices in an adjoining room, she pleads, "Daddy, don't go, stay here with me, watch over me" (185). And preparing to leave her lover she imagines that, "I'll be taken home to my mother and father on a stretcher, and they'll have to guess my wishes . . . and they'll sit next to my bed and read me stories" (219-20). Time after time in a variety of situations, Ya'ara longs for reunification with her parents as she fantasizes being cared for by them as though she were again a young child. "Mommy and Daddy" signify authority and hierarchy, a return to the comfortable certitude of childhood's earlier days. Ya'ara's yearning for what once was and is no more encapsulates her feeling of being trapped, without a present or a viable future. All that matters has already taken place. Ya'ara's dilemma is one faced by those who have not broken from a reified past, though the present they inhabit calls for far different responses.

A state of endless childhood is reinforced by the tight net of relationships that links parents, husband Yoni, lover Aryeh, and Ya'ara herself in an ongoing mutual dependency. Reviewing their situation, Ya'ara comments that, "now we all shared the same fate, Yoni who had lost his mother, I who had lost my brother and Aryeh who had lost his wife, we were all one big unhappy family" (168). And every member of this closely knit unhappy family is competing over whom is most grief-stricken, even as they share a combined fate. This family is living out a drama, all its players caught in an interwoven muddle. Holding together the dysfunctional morass is a kind of separation anxiety, a panic of letting go of past pain for fear of what might replace a familiar despair.

Certainly Ya'ara's choice of a lover is less an escape from the past than an attempt to wrench disparities into some order, to bring everyone together in a crazy quilt of interdependence. With old family friend Aryeh as her lover, Ya'ara fantasizes that the long-standing bond between her parents and this man will protect her: "my being here [with Aryeh] seemed less absurd, and also less frightening, after all he was a friend of my father's, he wouldn't really hurt me " (182). And when, still hidden in Aryeh's bedroom, she hears the three old friends talking together, she says, "I enjoyed listening to them talking without tension or bitterness, like a little girl whose parents have made up and she can go to sleep secure in the knowledge that when she wakes up in the morning she will find both of them at home, in a good mood" (225). The familial associations are underscored time and again, parents and lover merging into a parental unit for this girl-woman. This is underscored by Aryeh who repeatedly refers to his young lover Ya'ara as "Korman's daughter," (14, 57, 79, 246) —placing her squarely in the context of being child to his old comrades.

The tangled web of misalliances illustrates confusion of a high order. No one in this circle is capable of making informed choices. Rather the mutual entanglements point to a chaos that can arise when roles within domestic arrangements are seriously confounded. Early Zionism envisioned men and women free to live fuller erotic lives unbound by ugly remnants of the past. But Shalev's people lead erotic lives that are a mess, snared in a shared history which they are incapable of modifying to face a reconfigured present. At best, the sexual relationship between Aryeh and Ya'ara is Eros subdued; at worst, it is Eros perverted into a mechanized dumb show. Ya'ara asks herself, "how could I have failed to realize that he was completely dependent on my dependence on him, that this was the only thing he wanted" (269).

At some point, Ya'ara realizes how absurdly futile matters are: " [Aryeh was] keeping me hidden as if I were a backward child, or a demented wife . . . and suddenly I realized the full horror of my new status as a nonexistent woman who couldn't change her situation or even know it . . . and had no idea if her fears were groundless or her hopes were groundless, and who was dependent on a man who chopped and changed" (192). Ya'ara has no idea of who she is or might become, and has allowed herself to be captured by an unreliable male. Hopelessness grows, incapacitating any ability to devise alternative scenarios.

Having left her husband and taken up with a lover, Ya'ara has forfeited socially sanctioned roles. No framing concepts explain to herself or her society how she fits into the larger world. The Israeli woman, including she of Zionism's early days, was primarily defined as someone's mother, sister, daughter or helpful, supportive wife. Not fitting into these categories can have dire consequences, even for today's supposedly liberated Israeli woman. In Ya'ara's case, it leads to invisibility, to a sense of not-being. Desperately she comments, "all of a sudden I had become unwanted . . . when you're not wanted, you shouldn't be heard breathing, because you haven't really got the right to exist" (197). Ya'ara feels close to annihilation, having lost or never having assumed the roles that confer social legitimization. Considering a return to past certainties, she sees herself "go[ing] home to squeeze myself back into the frame of the picture of my life" (248). The image she conjures is of reinserting herself into a familiar tableau, even though that is awkward and ultimately impossible. The road back may be blocked, but at least it was a path once trodden. There is no other road visible on the horizon.

Aryeh is a figure out of earlier Zionist visions, a hero like those in former days of the State's founding who sacrificed a great deal in defense of his country. A war injury left him sterile. Ya'ara's mother supposedly rejected him as a suitor because he could not bear children. The wound is interesting for the fact that it is invisible: "he didn't have a single scar . . . his severe wounds hadn't left a mark" (228). Like many serious damages, the injury is hidden though it is grave. Aryeh is an intensely sexualized being, and yet a part of him—one linked to traditional notions of masculinity—is permanently dysfunctional. And this grievous damage is the result of having served his country. The heroic Israeli warrior is now a man whose reproductive organs are dysfunctional, his generativity foreclosed.

But though Aryeh contributed to a vanished, supposedly superior earlier world—as one of its warriors—his status within the world he helped create is uncertain. It emerges that he is a dark-skinned, non-European Jew. This fact is never emphasized, with only occasional hints in Ya'ara's descriptions as when she remarks on: "his dark profile" or says "he looked to me like an Indian, with his brown skin and silver-gray hair and high cheekbones" (49). The fullest revelation of Aryeh's outsider status as a non-Ashkenazi Israeli comes when he himself tells Ya'ara, "I was a black kid from a slum, with a dubious past and uncertain future, not like your father with his European doctor parents. . . . his good education" (231).

Aryeh insists that his marginal status was the reason her mother rejected him. It was class and color, not sterility, that led to his being rebuffed. For Ya'ara, the history her lover recites is part of her parents' story, her need to tie together these three adults. But what Aryeh says is not a narrative for which she is prepared: "I was stunned, his story was so different from the story I had in my head" (232).

Tales she has been told throughout her young life are challenged by stories of this older lover. The clash of narratives is compounded by the generational chasm. Throughout their couplings, Ya'ara remains acutely aware of the fact that "the face of . . . old age . . . had pounced on him with unsheathed claws, as if in any case he would soon die of cardiac arrest right here in front of me" (24-25), and she refers to him at one point as "a gloomy old man" (38). Sex is linked with age, decay and death. Eros is perverted into a preoccupation with mortality. Ya'ara is caught in an ongoing battle: the forces of the past threaten to maroon her in a dying place, and a fearful future holds no promise except terrible emptiness. Lover and parents are life-long friends constituting a triangle blocking all exits. And stories explaining the past, tales she has relied on, turn out not to be totally true; the adults upon whom she depends appear to be hiding critical facts.

Youth contending with age is a major component in her affair, the struggles of a junior person seeking both connection to and freedom from the past. Like her parents, Aryeh is a member of the generation that peopled Israel during a time of less fraught associations with founding Zionist ideals. As the lover of her parents' childhood friend, Ya'ara is re-enmeshed in their more hopeful narratives. Ironically, her love affair returns her to a child's world rather than that of an autonomous adult. Ya'ara reports that in her first physical encounter she "tried to avert my gaze, as if I had accidentally seen my father in his underpants" (15). As with marriage, her love affair is another instance of Eros gone awry. Unresolved conflicts beset a bewildered young woman caught in conflicting versions of who she ought to be, who she is and what constitutes her relationship with the past.

In her sexual adventures, lover and parents mentally merge. Inappropriate boundaries signal Ya'ara's immaturity as when she remarks of Aryeh, "I wanted to annex him, to know everything he was thinking every minute of the day, to be part of the things he thought about . . . and for there to be an overlap between his thoughts and mine" (129). In short, Ya'ara wants to lose her own identity and merge with her lover. Subsuming herself into him, she can forgo the need to think for herself. Confusion reigns as she tries to figure out her place in an unfolding story. Ya'ara's predicament is the dilemma faced by Israeli women who are both expected to act like men (i.e., join the army and defend the state) at the same time they are expected to nurture husbands and sons. The role conflict is puzzling and exhausting; no wonder Ya'ara wants someone else to figure things out for her.

Repeatedly, Ya'ara is entrapped as she lets herself be literally and figuratively pulled back into a connection with a bygone time that reduces her to an infantilized state. With no clear identity, she seeks to forge a sense of one through an inappropriate alliance. Old-time Israelis, like her parents and Aryeh, were heroes in a way denied to her. Their largeness diminishes as Ya'ara comes to know more about their stories. But puzzlement predominates as she questions what to make of her life, one lived outside the magic of earlier days. Old certainties may not work, but at least they offer the comfort of that which is familiar.

Her emptiness is pervasive. While sex between Aryeh and Ya'ara is powerful, it does not satisfy Ya'ara's continual hunger. Aryeh tells her, "you're so hungry and I'm so full . . . [and she says] I knew that he was right, I felt the hunger piercing me from inside, that was the word, hunger, not desire . . . because when you're famished you eat anything " (34). Aryeh, the old man, taunts his young lover; he needs nothing and he has nothing to give her who needs so much. Later she says, "you're thirsty for love, but what can you do, that's life, when you're thirsty you stay thirsty, nobody gives you a thing" (61). This mutation of erotic desire into something more fundamental— the pangs of hunger and thirst—underscores the privations under which Ya'ara feels buried. Eros is transformed into a basic struggle for food and water. It's a potent metaphor for a transformation of shattered dreams. Desire has been replaced by simple yearning to quench an unending thirst.

Not only has desire become more primitive; it has also become almost totally obliterated. Aryeh says, "I haven't got anything to give you [and Ya'ara] . . . responded enthusiastically, as if this were good news" (90). Frustrated desire welcomes the certitude of futility. The notion of Eros as a barometer of the national soul emerges. If we read Ya'ara as the new Israel and Aryeh as the old, the impasse reflects more than just a botched love affair. It is a metaphor for a lofty national purpose perverted into an empty, dead-end between warring participants. Where will Ya'ara/new Israel find nurture and renewal and when will Aryeh/old Israel remove the dead hand clutching past expectations that stifle present possibilities?

As the novel ends, Ya'ara finally begins to question her place in the narrative. In a bombshell revelation towards the book's conclusion, she learns that her mother never gave up desiring Aryeh; nor did Aryeh ever renounce his longing for his lover's parent. Ya'ara is a stand-in for each of them, a cipher through whom old attachments—and unresolved antagonisms—play out again. At first, she despairs as she senses how tightly bound she is in what she characterizes as "an ever widening circle of blame, encompassing almost the entire world, and how could I even imagine that it was possible for me to escape this circle" (233). Ya'ara feels implicated in what came before, in the mistakes made by parents and lover. But now she is no longer an inheritor of past glory; now she is part of its messy consequences:

> I had been . . . close to their youth, their past . . . I of all people had to change it, I who could barely move anything in the present, never mind the future. I of all people had to repair the past, because since it was spoiled I was spoiled too, and my only hope of coming right lay in putting it right, if it could not be put right neither could I. (227)

The enmeshment of the daughter/wife/lover in the unhappy betrayals of the past has shifted from that of innocent bystander to guilty accomplice. Ya'ara is desperate to find a way forward, both to redeem herself and to make right what has already taken place. The inchoate yearning of one generation to make amends and to reconfigure the past, the present and the future is a complicated notion of individual and societal redemption. It is, of course, not rational to believe that the past itself can be changed. But the consequences of past actions can be altered. Perhaps that is where redemption lies for Ya'ara.

While Ya'ara's future remains cloudy, she takes some faltering steps to extricate herself from the smothering grasp of the past. Making her way back to the university, wishing she could obliterate what has been, she murmurs, "Oh that I could go back to the beginning again, Oh that I could go back to the beginning again" (270). In relation to what has taken place, Ya'ara is "like a refugee, the survivor of a distant war coming face to face with her previous existence and fleeing from it, appalled, as if it were the enemy" (270).

But there is a modicum of hope; recognizing the futility of old mythologies creates space for new stories. Perhaps Ya'ara can write a new narrative, and perhaps her country can as well. First, though, she must look the past in the face. The novel ends with Ya'ara hiding in the university library all night as she clutches a book of legends, turning its pages and wondering about the sadness in the stories she's been told "when there was a power cut and the three of us were sitting around a single candle" (286). She's evoked this image before, in an earlier longing to go home again. Moving on is difficult, but finding a way forward requires more than a lone candle.

THINGS FALL APART (*HUSBAND AND WIFE*)

The second book in Shalev's (2000) trilogy, *Husband and Wife*, is a detailed account of the breaking apart of a conventional nuclear family consisting of husband Udi, wife Na'ama and only child Noga. The novel is a portrait of a disintegrating marriage as husband and wife discover to their dismay that a shared life is no longer tenable. The choices made by the protagonists as they face familial disintegration highlight agonies that are truly cross-cultural, though focus here is on the novel's relevance to fissures in Israeli culture. Present-day lives are collapsing under the weight of insupportable early hopes.

As in *Love Life*, the opening paragraph of *Husband and Wife* blasts readers with a sense that all is not well. Narrator Na'ama informs us that the first thing husband Udi says upon awakening is "even in a sleeping bag in the [desert] I slept better than here with you" (1). Things continue downhill as Udi retorts "angrily," "savagely," "resentfully". In front of their daughter who has come into the bedroom, he says "What do you need me for at all . . . you'd both be better off without me" (2). Husband and father is petulant, unhappy and self-pitying.

The situation immediately takes a dramatic turn towards the calamitous when he tells his wife, "I can't feel my legs, I can't move them . . . what is this blanket, it's so heavy . . . it's suffocating me, I can't breathe" (2-3). Wife

Na'ama reacts with disbelief and anger mainly directed at their daughter Noga against whom "a fist of revulsion presses me against the wall . . . and I scream, why are you making things even harder for me, I can't cope with you " (4). Throughout the narrative, Noga will be the target for much of her parents' misery. Wife and mother Na'ama will vacillate between rage and a dazed longing for the past connection she had with her now paralyzed husband.

Domestic things falling apart in this family reflect unendurable stress as traditional institutions like marriage and family fracture. Bodily breakdowns expose gaping fissures in people's lives, especially as individuals like Na'ama and Udi feel themselves in the grip of seemingly insurmountable chaos. Within the novel's contained universe of marriage, family and parenthood, a sense of an enveloping societal disorder plays out. Most significantly, the novel is a stunning illustration of how the new Jewish body envisioned by early Zionists came to be a decrepit, despised object. What happens to the physical entities of husband Udi and wife Na'ama is disheartening. For each of them, their bodies come to be sites of torment and dis-ease. These are not strong, heroic figures at home in a supportive, nurturing land. Here are broken people whose existences are unraveling as they struggle with seemingly intractable situations.

Na'ama senses the magnitude of the catastrophe immediately. Faced with her paralyzed husband unable to get up from bed, she realizes this is "the moment that breaks life in two, after which nothing is the same as it was before. . . . I can feel my life being drained out of me" (6). Thus concludes the first chapter, announcing that things are crumpling. All attempts to hold on to the family unit will fail. The sundering in their private lives has irrevocably altered everything. There was "before" when Udi could walk and there is "now" when he is deprived of mobility and mastery over his environment. The collapse of Udi's body is the end of much that held them together; it is also a metaphor for a broken dream of the Zionist desire for physical wholeness.

This body in free fall is that of "Newman Ehud, son of Israel . . . the popular tour guide, almost forty years old, married and father of one daughter, whose limbs refuse to obey him" (21). His narrator wife's description of Udi encapsulates a person emblematic of mythic Israeli elements. He is a native of the land, and by virtue of his work as a tour guide offers that land to others. Beginning with his surname—Newman—(new man) he handily represents the New Hebrew Man, lord of his native soil: His "legs never tired, guiding hikers in the Arava and the Judean desert" (2), and "Time after time he would go out on his hikes, sometimes completely alone, sleeping in tents in all kinds of godforsaken places, returning with shining eyes. . . . He never complained about floods, sandstorms, insect bites, he accepted it all with understanding as part of an intimate dialogue between himself and nature" (37).

Here's a male totally at ease in his inhospitable Israeli environment; nothing pestilent interferes with his command of the land over which he presides. Not only is Udi at home in Israeli mother nature, but he is fiercely independent: "always so rebellious, he never obeyed anyone, not his teachers in school or his officers in the army, and they always forgave him in the end" (23). Both as student and soldier, Udi relies upon his own judgment, paying no attention to authority of any kind. And he is endearing so that his disobedience never has negative consequences. The image of a strong, fearless, charming man at one with his surroundings and answerable to no one but himself is quintessentially masculine, not unlike cowboy heroes of the Wild West. The description links with the notion of the heroic Israeli pioneer male. For this man, the soil of Israel is his to do with as he likes. As described by one literary critic:

> In the core myth of Zionism, it is the figure of the male soldier-farmer that occupied center-stage. . . . In the gendered language of Zionism, the partners in this new grand passion are on the one side, the Land, as both mother and virgin bride, and on the other the heroic Hebrew male pioneer, who has returned to possess the Land or to be received back into its bosom. (Mintz 1997, 11)

When that man is no longer mobile, no longer master of the soil, it is a huge disaster and in this emblematic situation "the defeat of his legs [brings] down the building of his inner self" (23). There is no interior life to sustain Udi when his physical prowess is compromised. Witnessing his paralysis is to see an end game in which a once powerful prototype is transformed into a crippled dependent child. Old certainties as to the nature of a noble Israeli male disappear. Udi's paralyzed body is that of a defeated, conquered creature unsure of what it means to be a man. Not being able to stride over the earth is a catastrophe calling into question core aspects of his identity.

The symbolism of someone like Udi transformed into a dysfunctional human—one who upends the idea of male heroism—is underscored further by the diagnosis of his condition: there is nothing physically wrong. One of the doctors tells Na'ama, "it looks like conversive paralysis . . . when the body converts mental stress into a physical problem" (58). Soon afterward Na'ama remarks, "The perfect test results had exposed the deception, and now he was sentenced to wander in the ambivalent gray area between the sick and the healthy, belonging neither here nor there" (63).

For Udi as for many of his male counterparts, it is this no-man's land that is the least habitable. The ambivalence in his situation, the absence of clear black and white, is a sentence to be endured. How much easier it would be if the situation were clear; if he knew the enemy within his body he could face it. This ambiguity extends further. Whose body is this? Whose place is this? Where are the boundaries to be drawn? How shall I live if I am no longer strong?

Not only is the ambiguity difficult for Udi, but his illness is also a cause for shame. The word *ashamed* (italics mine) is evoked three times in one paragraph describing Udi's mental state as he exits the hospital:

> [H]e himself is *ashamed* of his disgraced body. . . . His eyes are frightened . . .
> he fingers the letter discharging him from the hospital, *ashamed,* like a child
> bringing a bad report home from school . . . burying his face in the sidewalk,
> [he is] *ashamed* of being seen in his disgrace, the hero who was carried
> proudly away on a stretcher, fighting a mysterious disease, returning home in
> disgrace. (64)

The shame is primal, a child like state of being unmasked and vulnerable. Furthermore, this sense of shame is exacerbated by the fact that the illness comes from a failure of nerve and not from the body's inability to perform for physical reasons. The absence of tangible reasons for his dysfunction connects Udi's condition to invisible realities as powerful as anything seen by the human eye. Like Aryehs' indiscernible wound which rendered him sterile, the hidden nature of these broken male bodies makes healing elusive if not impossible. The disability is even more shaming as their injuries render them impotent in worlds over which they once dominated.

Vision itself disappears as Udi becomes hysterically (though not permanently) blind and cries out in terror, "'I can't see,' he screams, his hands stretched out in front of him beating the drowsy air like a baby's . . . 'I can't see'" (95). He literally loses the ability to comprehend what is right in front of him, regressing to an infantile state. At its heart, the disease poses a mystery which cannot be solved easily if at all. Ambiguity is multiplied as confusion proliferates as to what happened and what repairs are now to be made. With no answers, this hero wants to hide from the eyes of all. Anyone who sees him would judge him weak after gazing upon his impairments, as for Udi the exterior world mirrors his internal appraisal. He is incapable of any response save panicked helplessness. Futility feeds Udi's anger, as he seeks to destroy the one person who sees him most intimately—his wife. It's bad enough to be a cripple; it's even worse to fall apart in front of a spouse's knowing gaze.

A context for Udi's feelings of shame may be partially located in Zionist myths which define those traits that constitute an ideal Israeli male. This idealized macho figure is much admired worldwide, linked for some with the notion of the survival of the Jewish people as dependent on Israeli masculinized strength. Centuries of persecution of the People of the Book has led to an insistence that Jews are now also people of the ready military response.

The Israeli soldier hero is a common trope promising security and safe passage for Jews.

As the feminist scholar Simona Sharoni (2005) writes, "By making national security a top priority, by grounding it in specific interpretations of
Zionist ideology and of the history of the Jewish people . . . the state has
offered Israeli Jewish men, especially those of European or North American
origin, privileged status in Israeli society. . . . the construction of Israeli
masculinity in Israel is linked to the militarized political climate in Israel and
in the region" (241). When we meet Udi, he has already done his military
service and is working as a tour guide in the desert. While he is no longer on
active duty status, this description of masculinity linked to perpetual militar-
ism applies to him. His current work as a guide in the harsh landscape of the
desert offers further images of the idealized Israeli male. Cultural Studies
scholar Ella Shohat (1989) observes: "the *Sabra* [native born Israeli] hero
was portrayed as healthy, tanned . . . presumably cleansed of all Jewish
inferiority complexes, a kind of child of nature, confident, proud and brave"
(291). This is certainly Udi if we are to believe Na'ama's description of him.
And now this particular child of nature, desert tour guide and ex-soldier, is a
man who cannot walk and has lost his vision as well.

Masculinity is at the heart of notions of what it means to be a New Jew. It
is a masculinity that rejects feminine weakness and insists upon subjugating
feminine sexuality. This sense of masculinity is partly dependent on expung-
ing the female other, whether the feminine is internalized or exists in the
person of an actual woman. While women serve to reenforce core elements
of masculinity, male domination requires that the feminine occupy a secon-
dary or tertiary space. In essence, the New Hebrew Man is to be a rebuke to
notions of the Jewish male as impotent and diseased. Repressing the inferior
female is in the service of securing an unassailable manliness. Furthermore,
mastery over the land belongs exclusively to the male Jewish pioneer. In an
important sense, the land is female. It awaits conquest by the arrival of the
manly hero.

The correlation between masculinity and casting off the feminine plays
out in the sexual relationship between Udi and his wife. Their sexual dance is
an enactment of the male need to discard what he sees as unworthy parts of
himself by projecting it onto the hapless female. Udi's sexual dominance
over Na'ama demonstrates his ability to exert power and control. In their
sexual dance, wife Na'ama is the femininized, weak land which virile husband Udi conquers and upon which he casts out his own despised feminism.
There is, in short, a conflation between masculinity, virility, the triumph over
geography on one hand and femininity, weakness, and the conquered land on
the other.

In their relationship, sex was one of the chief elements that held Udi and
Na'ama together. This sexual energy was a constant by which Udi reinforced

his maleness. But as things fall apart, Udi's sexuality shifts from impotence to a brutalized kind of physical conquest to a blunt-edged weapon with which to beat his wife and accuse her of making him sick. Sexuality begins to turn ugly when Na'ama writes, "I stand in front of him naked, not the provocative, impulsive nakedness I once possessed, natural and confident as that of an animal, but a human, apologetic nakedness . . . [in which] it wasn't a loving eye that was glaring at me now " (9). "[It's] as if he's throwing stones at me from his bed, a gravel of filthy syllables" (12).

In her frantic attempts to repair matters, Na'ama doesn't pull back from sexuality. Rather she desperately tries to enlist it, hoping to bring Udi back by reinforcing his sexual prowess: "I lay my hand on his sleeping penis. . . . I can always depend on it, a faithful ally in a country that has turned its back on me" (68). In her desperation, a connection to sexuality via her husband's penis is what she counts on to restore order. Later, Na'ama "found myself appeasing him all the time, trying to prove to him . . . that I had chosen him wholeheartedly . . . and . . . this turned into my life's mission" (92). Seeking to reassure her husband, Na'ama represses any part of herself that might interfere with her husband's need to reexperience dominance. Recognizing Yudi's need for mastery, Na'ara comments on a temporary reprieve after they make love: "it seems as if all our lives we have been striving for this renunciation . . . his fierce desire, it's me he wants and what could be better, it's mastery he wants and what could be easier . . . the fire of an ancient, painful covenant . . . consuming all doubts . . . if you are true to it no harm will come to you" (94).

The declension is clear: rejected woman uses sexual arousal to achieve connection in a way that is tried and true and ancient; if the penis works, the marriage will survive. If the marriage survives, the world will be put right. If the world is put right, the old narratives will hold sway—the ancient covenant will be reasserted. Udi's need for mastery over Na'ama and all the feminine aspects she represents will once again consume all doubts. Na'ama is willing to subjugate herself in the interest of restoring Udi to a sense of untrammeled masculinity, returning him to the dominant position which is his only viable stance.

The sexual charge is ignited, but it doesn't burn for long. In fact, sexuality becomes totally perverted as Udi comes to view it as something sinister. Most damning, he insists that carnality is at the root of his illness. Na'ama's desirability is destroying him. "Leave me alone . . . I don't need your embraces . . . it's you who troubles me all the time, it's because of you that I'm sick" (96). This accusation is bad enough, but it gets worse as Udi continues his diatribe: "this morning it became clear to me that it's all because of the wasted seed, that's why I'm sick . . . you squeeze the sperm out of me, I can't go to bed with you anymore, the sperm is the essence of life, and I let you drink up my life with all the lips of your body" (97).

This is sexual hysteria of a high order, a total demonization of sexuality with the insistence that evil destruction lurks in the loss of precious male bodily fluids. It's another nail in the coffin of the idea of a healthy male Jewish body, the fear of a loss of sperm unleashing a fear of death. The waste of fluids relating to his sexual organ poses an existential threat to Udi's very being. Most striking, it's the New Jewish Man insisting he has been undone by the power of the despised, malevolent feminine. Udi curses Na'ama as the cause of his fall from potency, the reason he is a decrepit, dysfunctional male. She, like Eve with a clueless Adam, is the reason for his undoing.

This perversion of sexuality is one aspect of the metaphor of disease which figures so prominently in the novel, afflicted Jewish bodies becoming symbols of shattered dreams. From Udi's first terror at his paralysis to Na'ama's increasing abnegation of her own body, the impact of disease doesn't let up. Na'ama even gets to the point of personifying dysfunction, remarking "there has to be some cure for this collection of symptoms, and apprehensively I remember the name of his disease, Conversion [hysterical conversion], as if I've suddenly remembered the name of the other woman" (111). For her, disease has become a rival for the affections of her husband, as real as any person.

On his part, Udi is completely taken over by his dis-eased state, and Na'ama "forget[s] to ask him how he is, because it doesn't make any differ-ence anymore . . . the same devastating incapacity seems to be floating through his body . . . what has taken over here is the general tone, the sum of all the details . . . [he is] becoming addicted to this illness" (110). A feeling of well-being is supplanted by a never-ending state of sickness. Most distress-ing, Udi's surrender to his maladies leaves his wife to ponder an unchanging landscape of misery. She is as powerless as is her husband to make things right again.

The situation with Udi and Na'ama is a negation of all that is life-giving. Everything is perverted, from their sexuality to their basic general health, to their feelings about the bodies they inhabit, to the bonds that knit them together, to their relationship to the soil. As Na'ama says, "every feeling is contradicted by another feeling which negates it . . . until the love rots . . . a stinking swamp swarming with mosquitoes, and the attraction which some-times flickers like the glimmering of a delightful memory is repulsed by the aversion . . . I grow a hard shell around my heart" (112-3). It's the end of a dream of a meaningful life as Israeli man and woman, and there is no sense that anything will take its place. Aversion has replaced attraction, and the heart shrivels as desire dies.

Extinction of desire between husband and wife is one ending, as is death of desire related to the land. Udi's current connection to the land is epito-mized by his occupation as desert tour guide and in descriptions of his total ease in that hostile environment. There is also a compelling spiritual element between Udi and the earth, one observed by Na'ara remarking, "among the trees I see a pale figure swaying in dancing steps, flitting from tree to tree, and then kneeling, bowing down to the ground, as if in some ancient rite" (103). Here is Udi in a quasi-religious connection to his surroundings, worshipping in a kind of demented pagan rite.

When he and Noga take a long trip together, the land emerges more fully as a narrative element that links sexuality amongst these individuals to a lust for the soil itself. And like their shattered marital bond, the allure of the once desired land is broken beyond repair. Connection between person and place is most pronounced in scenes occurring after Na'ama and Udi have had a sexual encounter. A coalescence between their bruised sexuality and a particular locale turns their land into a mirror of dysfunction; ultimately it is a killing ground. Just after they have made love Na'ama ruminates: "the difference between inside and out suddenly blurred. . . . I [heard] the whisper of the steam like the steam of a furnace rising from the overthrown land, seeing the corpses of the ruined, smoking cities, the destroyed garden of God" (70). Udi takes this further, commenting that "I will never recover, even though thousands of years have passed it seems as if nothing has changed there, the sin was so deep that that ground can't heal, it was punished by eternal barrenness" (70).

Both husband and wife describe their environs as a place of death, a far cry from the desired land of earlier times. Sex is that ancient deep sin, an affront to God's garden. The accumulated insults have rendered the soil barren forever, with their lovemaking as the final blow. This absence of generativity, the destroyed garden, makes itself felt inside Na'ama as the boundaries between inside and outside blur in her mind. Destruction is evident in the violence of the sexuality between husband and wife. Na'ama is the feminized other, conquered by the strong Israeli male. Driving through this place, Udi has "his hand inside [Na'ama] and his eyes on the road. Come, he says through his teeth, I'm not stopping until you come." (79- 80). Udi prevails, brutally mastering Na'ama in his insistence on a sexual response. It is a sexual act which serves only to highlight the absence of connection save that cruel one which stems from male dominance over a trapped female. It is the opposite of sex as a sanctified act, the covenant that Na'ama envisioned.

What was to be a place of milk and honey, a bountiful, life-giving place, is gone. Na'ama describes "slid[ing] down the great asphalt chute into the dry arms of the desert . . . the land is one and the same wherever I look, salty, moonstruck land" (75-76). After their harsh sex, it seems to Na'ama "as if this wild landscape is visiting my bed . . . as if I'm lying on the bed of an ancient, salty, oily sea, close to the savage inner life of this land, to the footsteps of the wild animals who prowled here thousands of years ago" (79). The place where they copulate is a desolate, dangerous place suggesting savagery and ugliness. It is a far cry from the land desired by early Zionists in love with its possibilities.

Shortly after the imposed sex, Udi asks Na'ama if she wants to see a nearby necropolis. Startled, she asks, "an entire city of the dead?" (82). Udi replies, "yes, a burial city, from all corners of the Jewish world they came to be buried here" (82). Visiting this ancient burial ground, the environs darken further as they drive away and Na'ama comments that

> a dense mist bars our way and we twist and turn with the narrow road over mountains of cloud, at close quarters their touch is strange and hostile . . . and beneath us the deep, hungry abyss breathes heavily. A black rain suddenly pours down . . . already I can feel the tug ropes of the abyss . . . while above my head the magnet of the dark sky rules, one more snatched breath and the eternal balance of terror between heaven and earth will be disrupted, and I will be left suspended in nothingness. (83-84)

This is a powerful link between the state of the land, the darkness of the day and times, and an individual sense of despair. As in T.S. Eliot's objective correlative, emotional, spiritual and psychological truths are perfectly mirrored in the surrounding landscape. Mist, clouds, rain all portend disaster and a plunge into something forbidding. They visit a place where the dead from all over the country are interred. At the moment, terror is somehow held in check, but this precarious state may be shattered by a mistimed intake of breath. A great beast is slouching towards Bethlehem in today's Israel, and it is breathing right now on Na'ama and Udi and their land.

The proud, strong male *Sabra* [Israeli-born] Udi is one end of the spectrum. But the flawed myth of Zionism's New Hebrew Man raises the issue of what Zionism's New Hebrew Woman might look like. This is a more vexing question than it might initially seem. Early images of Israeli women suggested they were part of the project of building the new state as compatriots of their male brothers. Current notions of women's role and place in Israeli culture are less clear. Representations in text offer contradictory images of what a fully vested contemporary Israeli woman might be. While playing central roles in such institutions as the army and the government, and while themselves often internalizing macho values, women lack a central defining position within the strictures of a normative male-defined universe.

Na'ama is clearly a woman trapped within a phallocentric system. The foundations of it were laid out in founding Zionist stories which privileged the new Hebrew man without limning any compelling vision of the new Hebrew woman. The situation has become no better over the years. Na'ama surely derives her most marked identity from her role as Udi's wife. Yes, she is mother to Noga, daughter to her own unnamed mother and deceased father, and valued social worker in a home for young women who are giving birth to so-called illegitimate children. But none of these identities has the power to define and destroy her as does that of being wife to Udi. Women are still expected to be supporters to their men and keepers of the homefront. They may sometimes step out of these roles, but their core identities continue to depend on their status within a world where men are privileged.

Na'ama's central reference point is her marital relationship, even though things have long been difficult between her and Udi. She often refers to them as "husband and wife," as though this were one word. Husbandandwife subsumes all other realities, encompassing everything of value within her known world. The disintegration of this unit is the end of that which contains and defines her. Na'ama's distress is that of a woman overwhelmed by a sense of abandonment so severe it threatens to destroy her as a functional human being.

Na'ama's near self-destruction occurs in the aftermath of the perceived catastrophe she endures when her narrative is irrevocably destroyed. All the stories she has been told insisted on the role of wife as central, enduring position. Female Na'ama is terrified by the loss of this male who is all in all to her. The first desertion stems from his altered state when he is no longer physically whole. The abandonment is completed when Udi announces that he is leaving her. No matter how damaged he is or how miserable she is, their unit is the rock upon which everything stands. The breakdown of their relationship is not how things are supposed to be; it is not how the story was supposed to end. The demise of her marriage is the desolation of all meaning, and Na'ama strikes out against her own body. Violently turning against herself is more tolerable than looking at the black hole left by her now absent mate. Suffering massive feelings of abjection, she comes to perceive herself as less than human.

For increasingly as Udi withdraws from her, Na'ama becomes further and further marginalized, a wretched human being. Her abjection begins with Udi's efforts to expel those elements of himself he most fears, his feminine self. Internalizing Udi's insistence on her pollution, Na'ama sees herself as the weak, despised, female other. Her descent into self-loathing reflects a woman with no sense of herself except as a despised appendage. In addition, Udi's cruel rejection serves as a reminder of how an attempt to forge a new identity—in this case, a male Jewish identity free of the notion of being a despised, pathological, feminized other—is turned against his wife. Udi is the New Hebrew Man unbound by negative stereotypes. He has found someone upon whom to cast out undesirable traits—his female intimate. Udi and Na'ama are both casualties of a vision gone wrong. In addition, as Udi's immobility cuts him off from his primal connection with the land, he transforms this loss into hatred of his wife. She becomes, among other symbols, a land no longer pure. The land is dark and corrupt, as is his once beloved mate.

Na'ama's quintessential moment of abjection occurs just after Udi leaves their life. She sees herself as a toilet, literally something to be pissed on: "He won't pee here anymore, I tell the open mouth of the toilet bowl that swallowed his waters day after day, year after year, staring at him submissively as he stood before it with an unsheathed penis frothing its jaws with golden showers, he'll have another toilet to urinate in, and already its insult merges inseparably with mine" (206).

It's difficult to imagine an image more abject than one in which the abandoned wife identifies herself with the no-longer-needed recipient of her husband's urine. But Na'ama continues her litany of self-hatred and goes on abusing herself:

> I wash this body with disgust, a rejected body, what has it to do with me, for it was Udi who always mediated between us, it was he who loved it and now without his mediation it is alien to me, even soaping it makes me shudder, the prickly armpit sagging to the heavy breast, the belly that was once taut and is now flabby, the full thighs and the great dread between them, and finally the flat feet, broad as a duck's. (207)

Na'ara's self disgust horrifies with its relentless catalog of perceived physical decay. Calling her vagina a great dread suggests her acceptance of the link between Eros and death. Without her husband's gaze—his mediation—Na'ara is reduced to aging, ugly bits and pieces devoid of even the capacity to experience trauma. Her feet are so repugnant and her senses so dulled that, "[In the shower] I aim an almost boiling stream of water at them, and they hop frantically as if on blazing sea sand, but I don't care, their pain is not my pain . . . between the pain at the bottom of my body and the pain at the top are only a shaky scaffolding, rusty nails, the filth of humiliation" (207). Scalding water with seared skin is easier to endure than odious notions of her own physicality. Like offal, her body is fit only to be discarded. When the New Hebrew Man falls apart and disowns the New Hebrew Woman, the wreckage is profound.

So great is Na'ama's despair that she experiences herself as no longer human; in her self-loathing, she is transformed into a savage animal or even an insect. Saying farewell to Udi, she "rage[s] like an animal, kicking, cursing . . . follow[ing] him to the bedroom like an obedient dog" (199). Later she is "a snail without a shell, a soft, slimy slug" (207). Sometimes she is even less than an insect, reduced to a mechanical object as she describes being "a dirt truck that has emptied its contents and is looking for a new load" (248). Another time, meeting with a lover, "he's the tow truck and I'm the damaged car attached to his rear" (260). Surely no one could destroy her as effectively as she herself does. The ruination began with the demise of Na'ara's marriage, but its monstrous power owes something to the absence of any alternative way of envisioning her life outside the status of wife. Na'ara exists only insofar as she is linked to Udi, the man whose power to shape everything leaves her with no room to do the same. Rage against injustice, from her husband and from her culture, are transformed into coruscating self-abnegation.

And yet this Israeli woman continues to cling to the dream promised by betrothal and marriage. Even as things disintegrate, she asks,

> [H]ow could he leave, simply get up and go with his pack on his back . . . as if I were some site on a dusty map that could be abandoned, a dried-up creek he left behind in order to search for a better one, taking with him all I had, all I thought I had . . . what he's done is clearly illegal, people can get thrown into jail for less, abandoning a wife and child after so many years . . . it never occurred to me that it could end. (207)

In Na'ama's psychic landscape, it's impossible to see life beyond this dissolution, unimaginable to find alternative sustenance. Udi's desertion is a fundamental affront to the notion of any order in a world as portrayed through guiding narratives. In every conceivable way, everything is defined by how Na'ama stands in relation to her husband. Rhetorically she asks, "What will become of me now, I've never been alone, I was always with him, against him, for him, opposite him, underneath him, on top of him, behind him, I always tested myself in relation to him. . . . I'm a woman without a man, a woman without justification, anyone can humiliate me" (209-11).

Later she "feels . . . [being abandoned] keenly, how it was torn from my hair, ripping off pieces of my scalp" (243). It's a woman literally coming apart as she howls in pain and experiences a shredded self bereft of all sense of safety. All is over as she stands naked and afraid in a world not of her own making. Without her status as wife to Ehud (Udi) Newman, son of Israel, there is no grounding for Ya'ara Newman, daughter of Israel.

One final image of Na'ama and Udi may serve as a metaphor for much that has gone wrong with the founding Zionist dream of liberation, replaced by a sense that Israel and its citizens are continually under siege. N'a'ama describes their family as, "the three of us in one room, in one bed. . . . we had become, close and dependent, isolated as a forgotten tribe, hiding our treasure as if it were stolen" (42-43). Later, using the same intimate image of bed, she recounts, "All of us together in one room, on one bed, as if outside the room a war is waging and we're in hiding . . . fall[ing] asleep I see . . . a shape reminiscent of some distant land, almost empty of inhabitants, a conquered, suffering land" (66).

It's a sad image of people in enormous painful isolation, husband and wife cast adrift. Shalev's men and women have lost their moorings. The loss expresses itself in personal disconnections, and therein lies sadness enough. But larger disorientation stems from a sense of lost cultural narratives. Personal histories are inevitably affected by societal constraints. These families have indeed lost the plot. That plot was based on solid family life in a relatively secure social environment. That environment has proved to be treacherous. Inhabitants of the wild landscape described by Na'ama are continually assaulted by malevolent forces seemingly beyond their control. Maintaining a steady course that avoids the shoals of marital disintegration proves impossible in an environment grown ugly and disheartening.

Conclusion

Towards New Narratives

> Thinking about literature can help in thinking about politics. But thinking
> about literature is a very difficult process.
> (McDonald 1997, 4)

The master narrative of the Jews changed irrevocably with the founding of
the State of Israel. No matter what happens in coming years, the world will
never be the same for the Jewish people as it was before 1948. The eight
novels considered in these pages reflect elements of an altered story, record-
ing quotidian life in what was to be a blessed place. As Sidra DeKoven
Ezrahi (2000) suggests, "The question . . . [is] whether (particular) space as
the manifestation of holiness replaces the text that has served as its surrogate" (19). DeKoven is referring to the myriad of texts written by Jews
during centuries of exile, when books rather than physical space were what
she calls the center of gravity for the construction of homeland.

Actual settlement of the land of Israel replaced the yearning for it, dis-
lodging the primacy of the written word as the predominant grounding of a
universal Jewish home. This altered condition, the movement from exile to
corporeal home, is the background for the imagination of these writers. They
inhabit a modern nation-state, though one still viewed by many as the alleged
spatial manifestation of holiness longed for in ancient texts. Their novels
suggest the need for modified narratives, challenging long-held assumptions
of what "coming home" means. The presence or absence of sacredness in
their worlds is located in the vagaries of everyday life. It is not a built-in
component of a sanctified space.

This book is an invitation to look anew at Israel as a country unprotected by the notion of exceptionalism. The work surely does not challenge agonizing facts of Jewish history, the reality that the centuries have seen Jews repeatedly murdered and exiled. Having a homeland attempts to forge safety and to foreclose a repeat of earlier catastrophes. But *Death of a Holy Land* makes an implicit argument, based on a reading of Kaniuk's work, that relying on memories of the cataclysmic Holocaust to justify a militaristic public policy is misguided at best.

Neither does this work deny the perspective of those who wish to invest Israel with a quality of holiness, a sense of a place promised by an ancient covenant. The challenge of such an investment is to balance deeply held beliefs with the competing assertions of others, and to consider that holiness may be an attribute created by the human imagination. The ultra-Orthodox in today's Israel appear incapable of acknowledging any realities save those they insist upon, and for which they make a theocratic case. Fundamentalism in the nation is a powerful force in and of itself. In addition, it provides cover for less religious ideologues who use this essentialism to defend their own intransigent positions.

Over the centuries, a body of collective memory has formed to interpret the historical experience of Jews. Many (though not all) Jews throughout the world look to Israel as the embodiment of a long-standing promise of return to a place that gains its legitimacy from ancient, sacred records. But fulfillment of the dream of a Jewish homeland marks the beginning of a new set of challenges. When a religion and a nationalism merge, as they do in what is called the Jewish homeland, the results are problematic. Israel is an ethnocracy, a nation in which (Jewish) ethnicity gives favorable preference to Jewish citizens in the allocation of key rights and resources. Can such an ethnocracy make room for a more inclusive cultural framework or does the insistence on maintaining a Jewish state foreclose other options for the development of a more pluralistic vision of national identity? This is but one of many questions. The emotion surrounding discussion of Israel makes it hard to frame issues in the context of the land as a modern nation-state, with all that implies. It's impossible to predict when a shift towards normalcy—a time when public debate around Israel is less fevered and its world status less central—will occur.

Implicit in these non-canonical texts is an exhortation to reappraise cultural givens. Each artist offers perspectives on what life in Israel is like in reality rather than in mythic constructs. In their fictive worlds, characters struggle to make sense of what is happening to and around them. They grapple with complications of their own making as well as those arising from circumstances beyond their control. The power of these stories comes from the writer's skill in crafting a universe engrossing in its own right, regardless of theoretical interpretations by readers in search of existential meaning. But an exegesis of these novels yields a composite picture of a deeply troubled land, of lives playing out in a country enmeshed in old framing myths which block the need for narratives suited to changed circumstances.

Text itself is a fundamental element of Jewish life, the underpinning of core foundational beliefs. These artistic works deserve the esteem accorded untold amounts of text written over the centuries to explain Jews to themselves. Tradition holds that the Torah, as scholar Susan Handelman (1982) reminds, "was written with letters of black fire upon a background of white fire" (37). Respect for the illuminating fire in the writings of Kaniuk, Govrin, Castel-Bloom and Shalev has guided these interpretations. Honoring their text and the writer's integrity has been the first consideration. None of these novelists is writing a polemic; all are working in the interests of crafting a work of fiction worthy of serious consideration. As artists, they offer snapshots of reality, not solutions to seemingly intractable problems. History, as Shlomo Sand (2009) writes, "[is] among other things, an identity in motion" (22). These written preoccupations are part of the ongoing narrative of the Jewish people, an entity continually changing as forces both internal and external influence the nature of existence during any given period of time.

While overt political agendas are not articulated in these fictional works—though they may be inferred—it is noteworthy that Yoram Kaniuk recently won the right to list himself as "without religion" on the Israeli Population Registry, explaining that he had no wish to be part of a "Jewish Iran" or to belong to "what is today called the religion of Israel." Furthermore, Kaniuk remarked that "the Jewish religion has rejected the principles enshrined in Israel's Declaration of Independence.[1] It's too soon to determine whether Kaniuk's move to separate civic identity from a citizenship tied to religion is a harbinger of things to come or an isolated incident. Regardless of subsequent developments, such a bold move offers a clear alternative to the way national belonging is currently defined.

Commenting on Kaniuk's actions, historian and journalist Gershom Gorenberg (2011) goes further. He asserts, "The court affirmed a constitutional right to define oneself according to one's conscience—but only according to the inadequate categories of nationality and religion. Real freedom of conscience would require the state to stop registering religious and ethnic identity." Both Kaniuk and Gorenberg radically challenge the status quo. An Israel which separates religion from state and establishes a non-religious Israeli identity would be a major shift away from the notion of Jewish religious exceptionalism currently determining civil rights. It moves away from the framing concept of "holy land" towards a more pluralistic civic space.

Such a shift is not unrelated to a central assumption underlying this book. The country and its worldwide supporters need to grapple with Israel's standing in a global culture. Encouraging it to stand separately in a space defined as one protected by divine right makes near impossible the task of finding coherent compromises. As with its chief ally, the United States, a sense of divinely ordained exceptionalism obscures motives as it muddies individual and communal thinking. Shifting away from exceptionalism need not interfere with what may be called the Jewish character of this piece of the earth. Jews and Judaisms are many things, as is the case with the Israel that has been created from countless dreams. Not being a "holy land" removes one key part of a long-held equation. But it does not wipe away all that is of value nor does it erase a host of characteristics that may be placed under the general heading of Jewish culture.

Israel is a focal point for the world's attentions, and what happens in that part of the world has enormous significance all over the globe. Understanding the realities of life in Israel may assist in framing a new response to its policies. There is a great deal of vulnerability in that nation-state, often hidden under the appearance of certitude. The fictive citizens in these novels offer a glimpse of the fears and desires that lie beneath a sometimes bellicose exterior.

While this discussion has identified issues central to Jews and to Israelis in particular, the book's themes are universal preoccupations that transcend parochial concerns. Not only to Jews and their enduring stories do these novels speak. No matter the cultural label with which one identifies oneself, the writers address struggles inherent in the human condition. Furthermore, a close reading of text is not necessary to anyone for whom fiction offers delight, regardless of any so-called instruction. One can read Kaniuk for his perspectives on madness; Castel-Bloom for her satiric dexterity; Shalev for a meditation on love and its complications and Govrin for a look into the power of religiosity. All the works stand apart from the insights they suggest on life in contemporary Israel.

Judaism lays stress on the need to remember, to keep constant those associations that have made for Jewish civilization. The imperative to remember is sometimes at odds with the need to let go, to reframe issues in the light of new developments. Sometimes it takes as much courage to forget as to recall. Israel is not the place it was when statehood was declared in 1948. The world now is not what it was then, nor are Jews the same people as when exile was the only reality. Psalm 137 admonishes "If I forget thee, O Jerusalem . . . let my tongue cleave to the roof of my mouth." But what happens when Jerusalem forgets such imperatives as the need for compassion that must lie beneath any claim to the sacred? Reading Kaniuk, Govrin, Castel-Bloom and Shalev may be the starting point of a reinvigorated response.

NOTE

1. Zarchin, Tomer. 2011. "Israeli court grants author's request to register 'without religion.'" *Haaretz*. Feb. 2.

Afterword

This book grapples with questions regarding my sense of myself as a Jew. For much of my life, being Jewish was simply a given. If asked to use a limited number of words to describe my identity, the answer to the query "who are you?" would be "I am a Jew; I am a woman; I am an American." The last word is thrown in more for the sake of convention. I have never really seen my core identity as American, even though I was born and reared in the United States. I don't have a fixed sense of place, a location I call home without qualification. The closest feeling to home I ever had dwelled in my early infatuation with Israel, now a distant memory. Though I have lived in Northern California's Bay Area for over thirty years, I do not say of myself "I am a Californian." My primary identity is contained in the J word. And my Jewish identity is deeply tied to Israel, a connection increasingly fragile as Israel's government and its people move in a direction I find alienating.

As the bond I once felt is stretched to a breaking point, my increasing ambivalence may reflect the feelings of those for whom the Israel they envisioned has given way to a nation-state wracked by turmoil. In today's United States, the conversation about Israel is at a near hysterical pitch. Persons with differing perspectives are not only deaf to one another, but enraged with opposing points of view. One end of the spectrum tends towards a stance that justifies almost anything Israel does, shushing those who criticize it as either anti-Semitic or self-hating. Opposing viewpoints are finding a voice as the conversation shifts towards acknowledging the need for urgent change. But many of us who believe Israel must alter its course first have to work through fears of being labeled self-loathing as well as confronting an internal rage that threatens to choke us into silence. The anger partially arises from a sense of betrayal of early dreams.

For a second-generation American Jew of Russian and Polish ancestry, like many of my contemporaries, the founding of the State of Israel was to be the healing antidote to centuries of anti-Jewish slaughter culminating in the unspeakable Nazi Holocaust. For me as for other non-Israeli Jews, Israel would guarantee our personal and communal safety—forever. That Israel is now at the center of a Middle Eastern battleground as contributor to an ongoing state of unease; that it has turned out to be as damaged as any other nation-state; and that it is not the sanctified place I once thought it to be are realities that cause deep pain. For a long time, my imagined Israel was a magic place. Over the years, I visited a dozen times and felt the special link forged by communal associations. I went to Israel to study, to learn, and to find home. I reveled in the connections I made with the modern land and with the history that informed it. I ignored any voices that contradicted the sacredness of that space. Visiting during the second intifada, I boasted of being a few blocks from the stone throwing. What difference did Palestinian voices make to my sense of entitlement to this place? None. This land was my land.

There is a story that all of the Jews who ever lived or ever will live in the future stood together at Mt. Sinai to receive the Ten Commandments. I had an internalized vision of myself standing with them as part of this past, present, and future community of Jews. And while I did not believe a transcendent God would grant me eternal life, the connectivity I experienced led me back in time to my ancestors and forward in time to those Jews coming after me. I pictured myself on my deathbed rejoining a crowd of Jews huddled together in solidarity and warmth. I was part of a stream that had its source in an event thousands of years past with a promise of continuation into eternity. The Jewish world I inhabited had become central to a sense of safe belonging. Feeling at home like this was new to me, a balm to my soul. Home had become a place with a very Jewish address. And Israel was at the heart of my internalized Jewish neighborhood.

Thinking my way through a series of felt contradictions began when I chose a mate who is not a Jew. As one who intermarried, I experienced the end of a seamless relationship with an enveloping community. This loss of unquestioned belonging led to a reexamination of all I held dear. Jewish ritual and belief, ideas about the nature of the Jewish God, the Jewish idea of family, all came under my appraising gaze. And crucial questions arose around Israel. To reiterate, it is difficult to overstate the centrality that Israel played in my sense of Jewish selfhood. And now I felt the need to peer closely at it. What is this so-called holy land, both as symbol and reality? Who could help me see it as it is rather than as Jewish imagination has made it out to be? What exactly is the Israeli Jewish culture to which I am linked by age-old associations, and what concerns around meaning do its artists struggle to understand?

I turned to Israeli writers for insight on a central pillar of my belief system. Old narratives I had relied upon were turning out to be punitive and misleading. My feelings of exile didn't start with disillusionment around the Israel narrative, but this tale was entrenched in the self-identifying stories I told myself. Ruminations on my core identity as a Jew were partly based on Zionist master stories. The potency of the original dream, the enduring power of Israel as repository for core Jewish ideas of self, led to exploring my preoccupations through the works of people who live in that Israeli landscape. Through art, they seek to make sense of concerns both universal and particular. I came to challenge Israel's exalted status from a distance. Israel's writers grapple with its tensions as residents for whom this land is home. We meet in their books, linked by a desire to explore a place to which we are deeply attached.

Writing about Israeli novelists as an outsider offers a different perspective than if I were resident there. While hopefully many of the insights will resonate with readers who live in that country, my outsider status provides distance from the turmoil described. And though I do not inhabit Israel, its centrality in the psychic world of Jews gives me a stake in what goes on there. Writing as a U.S. Jewish citizen opens me to charges of being incapable of understanding what I don't know first hand, as well as charges of disloyalty. Right-leaning members of the U.S. Jewish establishment still insist that if you love Israel, you must unquestioningly support what the country does, and encourage the U.S. government to do the same. If I lived in Israel, some of this possible criticism might be leavened by that fact. But since being a Jew makes me part of a global community of my compatriots, I claim the right to speak without the need to take a loyalty oath.

Entering the conversation via this close reading of Israeli novels which I've read in their English translations, I bring particular biases. That is obvious, and I make no pretense of writing an objective study. But I have strived to base all observations on paying utmost attention to the craft in each of the works. I am distressed with attempts to stifle thoughtful critiques of Israel. The abuse hurled at recent books, articles and speeches questioning aspects of the nation is remarkable in its vitriol. Perhaps the intensity of the rhetoric is a measure of the fact that, like it or not, times are changing. Increasingly, Jews and their not unsympathetic supporters throughout the world are challenging the idea that Israel's actions must never be questioned. In Israel, vociferous debate continues; within the country itself there have always been vigorous voices in opposition to prevailing norms. The notion that Israel is too fragile to be critiqued is becoming an increasingly hollow construct. Jews are no longer hapless victims with nothing between them and catastrophe. Perhaps one major difficulty lies in recognizing the contradictions that come with power, rather than fearing the consequences that come with powerlessness.

But as I stated at the beginning, it is core issues of Jewish identity that engage and trouble me, that stimulate my creativity as they evoke a painful challenge to think clearly about matters that often feel overwhelming. An attempt to reflect soberly has motivated the time spent on this manuscript with the aim of interpreting the materials in a meaningful way. On my first trip to Israel, in the mid-nineteen eighties, I was asked for my Hebrew name. When I replied that I had none, I was told I could choose my own. I asked what I would be called if my name alluded to the notion of clarity, a lifelong pursuit made challenging by a none-too patient temperament. It was explained that the word for clarity in Hebrew is *brur*, and the appropriate female name based on that root is *Bruria* (which, as I learned later, was the name of a second-century female talmudic scholar). So in Hebrew I am called *Bruria*, and I hope I have done some justice to the meaning inherent in that name.

References

Aciman, Andre. *False Papers: Essays on Exile and Memory*. New York: Farrar, Straus, and Giroux, 2000.

———. *Out of Egypt: A Memoir*. New York: Farrar, Strauss, and Giroux, 1994.

Adler, Rachel. *Engendering Judaism: An Inclusive Theology and Ethics*. Boston: Beacon P, 1998.

Alcalay, Ammiel, ed. *Keys to the Garden*. San Francisco: City Lights, 1996.

Alter, Robert. *Hebrew and Modernity*. Bloomington and Indianapolis: Indiana UP, 1994.

Anidjar, Gil, ed. *Acts of Religion: Jacques Derrida*. New York: Routledge, 2002.

Armstrong, Karen. *A History of God: The 4,000 Year Quest of Judaism, Christianity and Islam*. New York: Alfred A. Knopf, 1993.

Arnold, Matthew. *Culture and Anarchy*. Ed. Samuel Lipman. New Haven: Yale UP, 1994.

Avineri, Shlomo. *The Making of Modern Zionism: Intellectual Origins of the Jewish State*. New York: Basic Books, 1981.

Avishai, Bernard. *The Tragedy of Zionism: How Its Revolutionary Past Haunts Israeli Democracy*. New York: Helois Press. 2002. Print.

Bakhtin, Mikhail. *The Dialogic Imagination: 4 Essays*. Ed. Michael Holquist. Trans. Kenneth Brostrom and Vadim Liapunov. Austin: U of Texas P, 1981.

Barker, Chris. *Cultural Studies: Theory and Practice*. London: Sage Publications, 2000.

Barthes, Roland. *The Pleasure of the Text*. Trans. Richard Y. Miller. New York: Hill and Wang, 1975.

Behar, Ruth and Deborah A. Gordon, eds. *Women Writing Culture*. Berkeley: U of California P, 1995.

Beinart, Peter. *The Crisis of Zionism*. New York: Henry Holt, 2012.

Ben-Ami, Jeremy: *A New Voice for Israel: Fighting for the Survival of the Jewish Nation*. New York: Palgrave Macmillan, 2011.

Benbassa, Esther. Trans. G. M. Goshgarian. *Suffering as Identity: The Jewish Paradigm*. New York: Verso, 2010.

Berg, Nancy E. *Exile from Exile*. New York: State U of New York, 1996.

Berlin, Isaiah. *The Power of Ideas*. London: Chatto and Windus, 2000.

Biale, David. *Eros and the Jews*. New York: Basic Books, 1992.

———. *Power and Powerlessness in Jewish History*. New York: Schocken, 1986.

Blanchot, Maurice. *Awaiting Oblivion*. Trans. John Gregg. Omaha: U of Nebraska P, 1999.

Bloch, Chana and Chana Kronfeld, trans. *Hovering at a Low Altitude: The Collected Poetry of Dahlia Ravikovitch*. New York: W.W. Norton, 2009.

Boyarin, Jonathan. *Storm from Paradise: The Politics of Jewish Memory*. Minneapolis: U of Minnesota P, 1992.

————. *Thinking in Jewish*. Chicago: U of Chicago P, 1996.

————. and Daniel Boyarin, eds. *Jews and Other Differences: The New Jewish Cultural Studies*. Minneapolis: U of Minnesota P, 1997.

Breslauer, S. Daniel. *Creating a Judaism without Religion: A Postmodern Jewish Possibility*. Lanham, Md: UP of America, 2001.

Bronner, Ethan and Isabel Kershner. "Israelis Facing a Seismic Rift Over Role of Women." *New York Times*. Jan 15,2012 World/Middle East.

Broucek, Frank J. *Shame and the Self*. New York: Guilford P, 1991.

Budick, Emily M, ed. *Ideology and Jewish Identity in Israeli and American Literature*. Albany: New York UP, 2001.

Bukiet, Melvin J, ed. *Nothing Makes You Free: Writings by Descendants of Jewish Holocaust Survivors*. New York: W. W. Norton and Company, 2002.

Burg, Avraham. *The Holocaust Is Over: We Must Rise from Its Ashes*. New York: Macmillan, 2008.

Caplan, Eran: *The Jewish Radical Right: Revisionist Zionism and Its Ideological Legacy*. Madison: University of Wisconsin Press. 2005.

Caputo, John D. *The Prayers and Tears of Jacques Derrida: Religion Without Religion*. Bloomington: U of Indiana P, 1997.

Castel-Bloom, Orly. *Dolly City*. Trans. Dalya Bilu. Paris: Loki Books, 1997.

————. *Human Parts*. Trans. Dalya Bilu. Boston: David R. Godine Publisher, 2003.

————. *Dolly City*. Trans. Dalya Bilu. Champaign: Dalkey Archive Press, 2010.

Castelli, Elizabeth A. and Rosamond C. Rodman, eds. *Women, Gender, Religion: A Reader*. New York: Palgrave, 2001.

Cisoux, Helene. *Portrait of Jacques Derrida as a Young Jewish Saint*. New York: Columbia UP, 2004.

Cleary, Joe. *Literature, Partition and the Nation State: Culture and Conflict in Ireland, Israel and Palestine*. Cambridge: Cambridge UP, 2002.

Cohen, Arthur. *The Myth of the Judeo-Christian Tradition*. New York: Harper and Row, 1969.

Cramer, Richard B. *How Israel Lost: The Four Questions*. New York: Simon and Schuster, 2004.

Culler, Jonathan. *Framing the Sign: Criticism and Its Institutions*. Oxford: Basil Blackwell, 1988.

Cupitt, Don. *After God: The Future of Religion*. London: Weidenfield and Nicolson, 1997.

Daiches, David. *Two Worlds, An Edinburgh Jewish Childhood*. Tuscaloosa and London: U of Alabama P, 1956.

Daniel, E. Valentine and Jeffrey M. Peck, eds. *Culture/Contexture: Explorations in Anthropology and Literary Studies*. Berkeley: U of California P, 1996.

Daniel, Jean. *The Jewish Prison: A Rebellious Meditation on the State of Judaism* . Hoboken, N. J.: Melville House, 2003.

Davies, William D. *The Territorial Dimension in Judaism*. Berkeley: U of California P, 1982.

de Vries, Hent. *Philosophy and the Turn to Religion*. Baltimore: Johns Hopkins UP, 1999.

Derrida, Jacques. *Acts of Religion*. Ed. Gil Anidjar. New York and London: Routledge, 2002.

————. and Gianni Vattimo, eds. *Religion and Cultural Memory in the Present*. Cambridge: Polity, 1998.

Docherty, Thomas. *Postmodernism: A Reader*. New York: Columbia UP, 1993.

During, Simon, ed. *The Cultural Studies Reader: Second Edition*. London: Routledge, 1999.

Eisen, Arnold. *Galut: Modern Jewish Reflections on Homelessness and Homecoming*. Bloomington and Indianapolis: Indiana UP, 1986.

Eliade, Mircea. *The Sacred and the Profane: The Nature of Religion*. Trans. Willard Trask. New York: Harcourt Brace, 1968.

Ezrahi, Sidra deK. *Booking Passage: Exile and Homecoming in the Modern Jewish Imagination*. Berkeley: U of California P, 2000.

Feldman, Yael S. *No Room of Their Own: Israeli Women's Fiction*. New York: Columbia UP, 1999.

————. "From The Madwoman in the Attic to The Women's Room: The American Roots of Israeli Feminism." *Israel Studies* 5.1 (2000). Accessed 28 Oct 2012. http://www.accessmylibrary.com/article-1G1-63131680/madwoman-attic-women-room.html.

Finkielkraut, Alain. *The Imaginary Jew*. Trans. Kevin O'Neill and David Suchoff. Lincoln: U of Nebraska P, 1983.

Foster, Hal. *The Anti-Aesthetic: Essays on Postmodern Culture*. Port Townsend, Wash.: Bay P, 1983.

Foucault, Michel. *The Foucault Reader*. Trans. Paul Rabinow. New York: Pantheon, 1984.

Freedman, Samuel G. *Jew vs. Jew*. New York: Simon and Schuster, 2000.

Freud, Sigmund. *Moses and Monothesim*. New York: Vintage Books, 1939.

Fuchs, Esther, ed. *Israeli Women's Studies: A Reader*. New Brunswick: Rutgers UP, 2005.

Fuery, Patrick and Nick Mansfield. *Cultural Studies and the New Humanities: Concepts and Controversies*. Oxford: Oxford UP, 1997.

Geisler, Michael, ed. *National Symbols, Fractured Identities: Contesting the National Narrative*. Vermont: Middlebury, 2005.

Gilman, Sander L. *Jewish Self-Hatred*. Baltimore: Johns Hopkins UP, 1986.

————. *The Jew's Body*. New York and London: Routledge, 1991.

Gluzman, Michael. "The Exclusion of Women from Hebrew Literary History." *Prooftexts* 11.3 (1991): 259-278.

Goldberg, David T. and Michael Krauz, eds. *Jewish Identity*. Philadelphia: Temple UP, 1993.

Gorenberg, Gershom. *The Accidental Empire: Israel and the Birth of the Settlements 1967 – 1977*. New York: Henry Holt and Co., 2006.

————. *The Unmaking of Israel*. New York: Harper Collins. 2011.

Govrin, Michal. *The Name*. Trans. Barbara Harshav. New York: Riverside Books, 1998.

————. *Snapshots*. Trans. Barbara Harshav. New York: Riverside Books, 2007.

Greenblatt, Stephen. *Renaissance Self-Fashioning: From More to Shakespeare*. Chicago: U of Chicago P, 1980.

Grindea, Miron, ed. *Jerusalem: The Holy City in Literature*. London: Kahr and Averill, 1968.

Grossman, David. "Rabin Memorial Ceremony," Rabin Square, Tel Aviv, Israel, 4 Nov 2006. Address.

Guttman, Nathan. "The Biggest Pro-Israel Group in America? That's Us, Says Christians United." *The Jewish Daily Forward*. Dec 17, 2010.

Halperin-Kaddari, Ruth. *Women in Israel: A State of Their Own*. Philadelphia. U of Philadelphia P, 2004.

Halpern, Ben and Reinharz, Jehuda. *Zionism and the Creation of a New Society*.New York: Oxford Univ. Press, 1998.

Hampl, Patrick. *I Could Tell You Stories: Sojourns in the Land of Memory*. New York: W. W. Norton, 1999.

Handelman, Susan A. *Fragments of Redemption: Jewish Thought and Literary Theory in Benjamin, Scholem, and Levinas*. Bloomington: Indiana UP, 1991.

————. *The Slayers of Moses: The Emergence of Rabbinic Interpretation in Modern Literary Theory*. Albany: SUNY, 1982.

Harb, Ahmad. "Representations of Jerusalem in the Modern Palestinian Novel." *Arab Studies Quarterly* 26 (2004). Accessed 28 Oct 2012. http://www.thefreelibrary.com/Representations+of+Jerusalem+in+the+modern+Palestinian+novel-a0129016013.

Hart, Kevin. *The Dark Gaze: Maurice Blanchot and the Sacred*. Chicago: U of Chicago P, 1994.

Hartman, David. *Conflicting Visions*. New York: Schocken, 1990.

Hazelton, Laurel. *Israeli Women: The Reality Behind the Myths*. New York: Simon and Shuster, 1977.

Hever, Hanan. "Israeli Fiction in The Early Sixties." *Prooftexts* 10 (1990): 47-129.

Hillel, Daniel. *The Natural History of the Bible*. New York: Columbia University Press. 2006.

Hoffman, Anne G. "Bodies and Borders: The Politics of Gender in Contemporary Israeli Fiction." *The Boom in Contemporary Israeli Fiction*. Ed. Alan Mintz. Boston: Brandeis UP, 2007. 35-70.

————. "Complex Histories, Contested Memories: Some Reflections on Remembering Difficult Pasts." *Doreen B. Townsend Center for the Humanities. Occasional Papers.* 23 (2000). Accessed 28 Oct 2012. http://repositories.cdlib.org/townsend/occpapers/23.

Hoffman, Eva. *After Such Knowledge: Memory, History and the Legacy of the Holocaust.* New York: Public Affairs P, 2004.

Jabès, Edmond. *Desire for Beginning, Dread of One Single End.* Trans. Rosemarie Waldrop. New York: Granary Books, 2001.

Jacobson, David C. "Intimate Relations Between Israelis and Palestinians in Fiction by Israeli Women Writers." *Shofar: An Interdisciplinary Journal of Jewish Studies* 25.3 (2007): 32-46.

Jayyusi, Salma K, ed. *Anthology of Modern Palestinian Literature.* New York: Columbia UP, 1992.

Kahn, Lothar and Donald D. Hook. *Between Two Worlds. A Cultural History of German-Jewish Writers.* Iowa: Iowa State UP, 1993.

Kaniuk, Yorum. *Adam Resurrected.* Trans. Seymour Simckes. New York: Grove P, 1971.

————. *His Daughter.* Trans. Seymour Simckes. New York: George Braziller, 1988.

Kaplan, Neil. *The Israel-Palestine Conflict: Conflicted Histories.* Hoboken, NJ: Wiley-Blackwell. 2010.

Kellerman, Aharon: *Society and Settlement: Jewish Land of Israel in the Twentieth Century.* Albany: SUNY, 1993.

Kepnes, Steven, Peter Ochs, and Robert Gibbs. *Reasoning After Revelation: Dialogues in Postmodern Jewish Philosophy.* Boulder: Westview P, 2002.

————, ed. *Interpreting Judaism in a Postmodern Age.* New York: New York UP, 1996.

Keret, Etgar and Samir El-Youssef. *Gaza Blues.* London: David Paul, 2004.

Khazzoom, Loolwa, ed. *The Flying Camel: Essays on Identity by Women of North African and Middle Eastern Jewish Heritage.* Emeryville, CA: Seal P, 2004.

Kovell, Joel. *Overcoming Zionism: Creating a Single Democratic State in Israel/Palestine.* Ann Arbor: U of Michigan P, 2007.

Kushner, Tony and Alisa Salmon, eds. *Wrestling with Zion: Progressive Jewish-American Responses to the Israeli-Palestinian Conflict.* New York: Grove P, 2003.

Laor, David. "American Literature and Israeli Culture: The Case of the Canaanites." Israel *Studies* 5.1 (2000). Accessed 28 Oct 2012. http://muse.jhu.edu/journals/israel_studies/v005/5.1laor.html.

Laqueur, Walter. *A History of Zionism.* New York: Schocken. 2003.

————. and Barry Rubin, eds. *The Israel-Arab Reader: A Documentary History of the Middle East Conflict, Seventh Revised and Updated Edition.* London: Penguin P, 2008.

Lentin, Ronit. *Israel and the Daughters of The Shoah: Reoccupying the Territories of Silence.* New York and Oxford: Berghahn Books, 2000.

Lesch, Ann M. and Dan Tschirgi. *Origins and Development of the Arab-Israeli Conflict.* Westport, CT. and London: Greenwood P, 1998.

Liebman, Charles S. and Eli'ezer Don-Yiha. *Civil Religion in Israel: Traditional Judaism and Political Culture in the Jewish State.* Berkeley: University of California P. 1983.

Loomba, Ania. *Colonialism / Postcolonialism.* London and New York: Routledge, 1998.

Loshitzky, Yosefa. *Identity Politics on the Israeli Screen.* Austin: The U of Texas P, 2002.

Louër, Laurence. *To Be an Arab in Israel.* New York: Columbia UP, 2003.

Lynd, Helen M. *On Shame and the Search for Identity* (International Library of Psychology). London: Routledge, 1999.

Lyotard, Jean F. *Heidegger and "the jews."* Trans. Andreas Michel and Mark Roberts. Minneapolis: U of Minnesota P, 1990.

————. *The Postmodern Condition: A Report on Knowledge.* Trans. Regis Durand. Minneapolis: U of Minnesota P, 1979.

Macintyre, Donald. "Avraham Burg: Israel's New Prophet." *Independent* 1 Nov. 2008. Accessed 1 July 2009. http://www.independent.co.uk/arts-entertainment/books/features/avraham-burg-israels-new-prophet-979732.html.

Margalit, Avishai. "In Israel: A Moral Witness to the Intricate Machine." Rev. of *Dark Hope: Working for Peace in Israel and Palestine,* By David Shulman. *New York Review of Books* LIV.19 (2007): 34.

Matalon, Ronit. *The One Facing Us.* Trans. Marsha Weinstein. New York: Henry Holt and Co., 1995.

McDonald, Peter. *Mistaken Identities: Poetry in Northern Ireland.* Oxford: Clarendon P, 1997.

Mearsheimer, John and Stephen M. Walt. *The Israel Lobby and U.S. Foreign Policy.* New York: Farrar, Straus and Giroux, 2007.

Meyer, Stefan. G. *The Experimental Arabic Novel: Postcolonial Literary Modernism in the Levant.* New York: SUNY P, 2000.

Miller, Susan. *The Shame Experience.* Hilledale, N. J.: The Analytic P, 1985.

Mintz, Alan, ed. *The Boom in Contemporary Israeli Fiction.* Hanover, NH: Brandeis UP, 1997.

———. "Fracturing the Zionist Narrative." *Judaism: A Quarterly Journal of Jewish Life and Thought* 4 (2000). Accessed 1 Oct 2009. http://www.accessmylibrary.com/article-1G1-59120275/fracturing-zionist-narrative.html.

———. *Banished from Their Father's Table: Loss of Faith and Hebrew Autobiography.* Bloomington: Indiana UP, 1989.

Moi, Toril. *Sexual/Textual Politics: Feminist Literary Theory.* London: Routledge P, 1988.

Morrison, Toni. *Playing in the Dark: Whiteness and the Literary Imagination.* Cambridge: Harvard UP, 1992.

Neumann, Boaz. Land and Desire in Early Zionism. Waltham, Mass: Brandeis University P. 2011

Nusseibeh, Sari and Anthony David. *Once Upon a Country: A Palestinian Life.* New York: Farrar, Strauss, and Giroux, 2007.

Omer-Sherman, Ranen. *Israel and Exile: Jewish Writing and the Desert.* Urbana and Chicago. U of Illinois P, 2006, Print.

Oppenheimer, Robert. Interview. *The Decision to Drop the Bomb.* Prod. Fred Freed. NBC 1965. Television.

Peled-Elhanan, Nurit. *Palestine in Israeli School Books.* New York. I. B. Tauris. 2012.

Peraino, Kevin. "Israel's Glass Ceiling." *Newsweek* 24 Sept. 2008. Accessed 20 Oct 2012. http://www.thedailybeast.com/newsweek/2008/09/24/israel-s-glass-ceiling.html.

Plaskow, Judith. *Standing Again at Sinai: Judaism from a Feminist Perspective.* San Francisco: Harper, 1990.

Plaut, W. Gunther, Bernard J. Bamberger, and William W. Hallo. *The Torah: A Modern Commentary.* New York: The Jewish Publication Society, 1981.

Reinharz Jehuda and Shapira, Anita, eds; *Essential Papers on Zionism.* NY: NYU, 1996.

Richter, David H. *The Critical Tradition: Classic Texts and Contemporary Trends.* Boston: Bedford Books, 1998.

Rimmon-Kenan, Shlomith. *Narrative Fiction: Contemporary Poetics.* London: Routledge, 1983.

Robertson, Richie and Edward Timms, eds. *Theodor Herzl and the Origins of Zionism.* Edinburgh: Edinburgh University, 1997.

Rose, Jacqueline. *The Question of Zion.* Princeton: Princeton UP, 2005.

Rosenberg, Oz. "Woman in Beit Shemesh attacked by ultra-Orthodox extremists." *Haaretz.* Jan 25, 2012. News.

Ross, Angus and David Woolley, eds. *Jonathan Swift Major Works.* Oxford: Oxford UP, 1984.

Royle, Nicholas. *Telepathy and Literature: Essays on the Reading Mind.* Oxford: Basil Blackwell, 1990.

———. *Jacques Derrida.* London: Routledge, 2003.

Rubin, Derek, ed. *Who We Are: On Being (and Not Being) a Jewish American Writer.* New York: Shocken, 2005.

Sachar, Harold. *Diaspora: An Inquiry into the Contemporary Jewish World.* Philadelphia: Harper and Row, 1985.

Sadow, Stephen and Ilan Stavans, eds. *King David's Harp: Autobiographical Essays by Jewish Latin American Writers.* Albuquerque: U of New Mexico P, 1999.

Said, Mustafa Bayoumi and Andrew Rubin, eds. *The Edward Said Reader.* New York: Vintage, 2000.

Said, Edward W. *Culture and Imperialism.* New York: Vintage Books, 1994.

Sand, Shlomo. *The Invention of the Jewish People.* Trans. Yael Lotan. London: Verso, 2009.

Sartre, Jean-Paul. *Anti-Semite and Jew: An Exploration of the Etiology of Hate.* New York: Random House, 1995.

Schiff, Ellen. *From Stereotype to Metaphor: The Jew in Contemporary Drama.* Albany: SUNY, 1982.

Segev, Tom. *The Seventh Million: The Israelis and the Holocaust.* Trans. Haim Watzman. New York: Farrar, Straus, and Giroux, 1993.

———. *1949 – The First Israelis.* Trans. Arlen Weinstein. New York: Macmillan, 1998.

———. *One Palestine, Complete.* Trans. By Haim Watzman. New York: Henry Holt. 2001.

Shabtai, Yaakov. *Past Continuous: A Novel.* Trans. Dalya Bilu. New York: Overlook P, 2002.

Shaked, Gershon, ed. *Modern Hebrew Literature 2: (Re)Writing Love in Postmodern Times.* London: Toby P, 2005.

———. *Modern Hebrew Fiction.* Ed. Emily M. Budick. Trans. Yael Lotan. Bloomington: U of Indiana P, 2000.

Shalev, Zeruya. *Love Life.* Trans. Dalya Bilu. New York: Grove P, 1997.

———. *Husband and Wife.* Trans. Dalya Bilu. New York: Grove P, 2000.

Shavit, Ariel. "Leaving the Zionist Ghetto." *Ha-aretz* 26 July 2008. Accessed 1 Oct 2009. http://www.haaretz.com/hasen/spages/868385.html.

Shaw, Christopher. *The Imagined Past: History and Nostalgia.* Ed. Malcolm Chase. New York: Manchester UP, 1989.

Shindler, Colin: *The Triumph of Military Zionism: Nationalism and the Origin of the Israeli Right.* New York: Palgrave Macmillan. 2006.

Shohat, Ella. *Israeli Cinema: East /West and the Politics of Representation.* Austin: U of Texas P, 1989.

Shoshan, Boaz, ed. *Discourse on Gender/Gendered Discourse in the Middle East.* Westport, CT: Praeger, 2000.

Silberstein, Laurence J. *The Postzionism Debates: Knowledge and Power in Israeli Culture.* New York: Routledge, 1999.

Stanislawski, Michael. *Autobiographical Jews: Essays in Jewish Self-Fashioning.* Seattle: U of Washington P, 2004.

Stein, Rebecca L. and Ted Swedenburg, eds. *Palestine, Israel, and the Politics of Popular Culture.* Durham and London: Duke UP, 2005.

Sternhell, Zeev: *The Founding Myths of Israel: Nationalism, Socialism,and the Making of the Jewish State.* Trans: David Maisel. Princeton: Princeton UP, 1998.

Sternhell, Zev. *The Founding Myths of Israel.* Trans. David Maisel. Princeton: Princeton UP, 1999.

Todorov, Tzvetan. *Literature and Its Theorists: A Personal View of Twentieth-Century Criticism.* Trans. Catherine Porter. Ithaca: Cornell UP, 1987.

Tyler, Patrick. *Fortress Israel: The Inside Story of the Military Elite Who Run the Country—and Why They Can't Make Peace.* New York: Farrar, Straus and Giroux, 2012.

Viorst, Milton. *What Shall I Do With This People?* New York: The Free P, 2002.

Ward, Graham. *Theology and Contemporary Critical Theory: Second Edition.* London: Macmillan, 1996.

Wiegand, David. "Don't Call him a Jewish Writer." *San Francisco Chronicle* 30 May 2007: E3.

Wills, Lawrence M. *The Jewish Novel in the Ancient World.* Ithaca: Cornell UP, 1995.

Winslow, Peter. *Victory for Us Is to See You Suffer: In the West Bank with the Palestinians and the Israelis.* Boston: Beacon P, 2007.

Yerushalmi, Yosef H. *Zakhor: Jewish History and Jewish Memory.* Seattle: U of Washington P, 1982.

Zertal, Idith. *Israel's Holocaust and the Politics of Nationhood.* Trans. Chaya Galai. Cambridge: Cambridge UP, 2005.

———. and Akiva Eldar. *Lords of the Land: The War over Israel's Settlements in the Occupied Territories, 1967 to 2007.* New York: Nation Books, 2008.

Zerubavel, Yael. *Recovered Roots: Collected Memory and the Making of Israeli National Tradition.* Chicago: U of Chicago P, 1995.

Index

Abraham, xii, 21

Adam Resurrected (Kaniuk), 3, 4; Adam, as clown, 6; Adam, in concentration camp, 4, 5, 6; Adam, desert vision of, 12; Adam, and Commandant Klein, 12–13; Adam, madness of, 4–5, 6, 10; Adam, and Ruth, 5, 13; Adam, shame of, xv, 6; asylum in, 7, 8, 12; dog/boy relationship, 9–11; Germany, as home in, 5, 13; Holocaust, directly referenced in, xvi; Jenny, as disturbed, 8, 9; Jenny, as head nurse, 7; Jenny, and Hitler, as alike, 8, 9; Jenny, power of, 8; master-dog relationship in, 6–7, 8–9, 11

Adler, Rachel, 51, 53; dualism, 54

Arab Jews, xiii

Ashkenazi Jews, xiii

Auschwitz, 1

Ben Gurion, David, 23

Bethelem, xii

Biale, David, 70

Burg, Avraham, 2

Castel-Bloom, Orly, xi, xiii, xviii, 40, 43, 97, 98; allegory, use of by, 26–27; *Dolly City*, 23–24, 36; *Human Parts*, 36, 39; as invaluable voice, 42; inventiveness of, 25; as myth wrecker, 37; satire of, xvii; shame, as theme, in works of, xv; style of, 24; Swift,

comparison to, xvii, 24–25; wit of, 35, 36, 37, 38; See also *Dolly City* (Castel-Bloom); *Human Parts* (Castel-Bloom)

Christ, Carol, 56

Christianity, xii, 22

Christian Zionists, 21

Christians United for Israel (CUFI), 43n2

David, King, 21

DeKoven Ezrahi, Sidra, 95

Dolly City (Castel-Bloom), 23, 36, 37, 42; as allegory, 24, 26–27, 28, 36; body, as diseased in, 32; cancer, as metaphor in, 30, 32–33, 35; as comic masterpiece, 25; comic perversion in, 34; demented mothering in, 33; Dolly, as Israeli government, 26; Dolly, as Mother Israel, 27, 30; Dolly, as self-deluded healer, 34–35; Dolly City, as home, 28; Dolly City, and Jerusalem, as stand-in for, 24, 27, 28; Dolly and Son, meeting of, 26; Dolly and Son, as allegorical representation of Israel, 26; fear, as intoxicant in, 31, 33; hysteria in, 32; Israel, as dysfunctional place in, 24; Israeli life, satirizing of in, 23–24, 36; madness in, 28–29, 30, 32; map of Israel, carving of, on Son's back, 35; sex in, 32; shame in, xv; Son, as Israeli citizens, representative of, 26

Dome of the Rock, xii

About the Author

Rose L. Levinson, Ph.D. teaches courses relevant to Jewish identity at the University of San Francisco where she is adjunct professor. Active in contributing to dialogue around cultural shifts, she co-wrote *A Place in the Tent: Intermarriage and Conservative Judaism* which argues for inclusion of inter-married families in Jewish communal life.

Thinking from the margins informs her work as writer, radio host, teacher. As *Safta*, she occupies a contented center.